# First World War
and Army of Occupation
# War Diary
France, Belgium and Germany

29 DIVISION
86 Infantry Brigade,
Brigade Machine Gun Company
27 February 1916 - 31 January 1918

WO95/2302/6

The Naval & Military Press Ltd
www.nmarchive.com
**Published in association with The National Archives**

Published by

## The Naval & Military Press Ltd

Unit 10 Ridgewood Industrial Park,

Uckfield, East Sussex,

TN22 5QE England

Tel: +44 (0) 1825 749494

www.naval-military-press.com

www.nmarchive.com

*This diary has been reprinted in facsimile from the original. Any imperfections are inevitably reproduced and the quality may fall short of modern type and cartographic standards.*

© **Crown Copyright**
**Images reproduced by permission of The National Archives, London, England, 2015.**

# Contents

| Document type | Place/Title | Date From | Date To |
|---|---|---|---|
| Heading | WO95/2302/6 | | |
| Heading | 29th Division. 86th Infy Bde. 86th Coy. Machine Gun Corps. Feb 1916-1918 Jan. | | |
| Heading | 29th Division. 86th Infantry Brigade. Arrived Marseilles From Egypt 26th March 1916. 86th Brigade Machine Gun Company. 27th February to 30th April 1916. 1918 | | |
| War Diary | Suez | 27/02/1916 | 26/03/1916 |
| War Diary | Marseilles | 26/03/1916 | 27/03/1916 |
| War Diary | Port Remy. | 29/03/1916 | 29/03/1916 |
| War Diary | La Plouy. | 31/03/1916 | 31/03/1916 |
| War Diary | Beauval. | 01/04/1916 | 04/04/1916 |
| War Diary | Achieux | 05/04/1916 | 13/04/1916 |
| War Diary | Mailley Maillet. | 13/04/1916 | 30/04/1916 |
| Heading | 86 Bde M G Coy. Vol. I.II.III. 29 | | |
| Heading | 29th Division. 86th Infantry Brigade. 86th Brigade Machine Gun Company May 1916 | | |
| Miscellaneous | D.A.G. G.H.Q. 3rd Echelon. 1st June 1916 86th Coy Vol 4 | | |
| War Diary | Mailley Maillet. | 01/05/1916 | 31/05/1916 |
| Map | Trench Diagram 29th Div. Area. | | |
| Heading | 29th Division. 86th Infantry Brigade. 86th Brigade Machine Gun Company July 1916. Appendices attached:- Operation Orders. Casualty List. | | |
| War Diary | Auchion-Villers. | 01/07/1916 | 03/07/1916 |
| War Diary | Mailley Maillet. | 05/07/1916 | 06/07/1916 |
| War Diary | Acheux | 07/07/1916 | 31/07/1916 |
| Miscellaneous | 86th Machine Gun Company Casualty Roll to date. | | |
| Miscellaneous | No. 1 Section. | | |
| Miscellaneous | Head Quarters. | | |
| Map | | | |
| Miscellaneous | 86th Bde. Machine Gun Co. Operation Order. | 22/06/1916 | 22/06/1916 |
| Heading | 29th Division. 86th Infantry Brigade. 86th Brigade. Machine Gun Company August 1916 | | |
| Heading | War Diary of 86th Co. Machine Gun Corps. From 1st August to 31st August 1916. Volume 7 | | |
| War Diary | Brandhoek. | 01/08/1916 | 07/08/1916 |
| War Diary | Ypres. | 08/08/1916 | 29/08/1916 |
| War Diary | Brandhoek. | 30/08/1916 | 31/08/1916 |
| Heading | 29th Division. 86th Infantry Brigade. 86th Brigade. Gun Company September 1916 | | |
| Heading | War Diary of 86th Company Machine Gun Corps Vol 7. From 1st September to 30th Sept 1916 | | |
| War Diary | Brandhoek | 01/09/1916 | 09/09/1916 |
| War Diary | Ypres. | 09/09/1916 | 28/09/1916 |
| War Diary | Brandhoek. | 29/09/1916 | 30/09/1916 |
| Heading | 29th Division. 86th Infantry Brigade. 86th Brigade. Machine Gun Company October 1916. Operation Orders attached. | | |
| Heading | War Diary of 86th Company Machine Gun Corps from October 1st to October 31st 1916. Volume.8 Vol 9 | | |

| | | | |
|---|---|---|---|
| War Diary | Brandhoek. | 01/10/1916 | 04/10/1916 |
| War Diary | Herzeele. | 04/10/1916 | 08/10/1916 |
| War Diary | Daours. | 09/10/1916 | 10/10/1916 |
| War Diary | Dernacourt | 11/10/1916 | 12/10/1916 |
| War Diary | Mametz Wood. | 13/10/1916 | 14/10/1916 |
| War Diary | Mametz. | 15/10/1916 | 19/10/1916 |
| War Diary | Flers. | 20/10/1916 | 30/10/1916 |
| War Diary | Ville Sur Ancre | 31/10/1916 | 31/10/1916 |
| Operation(al) Order(s) | Operation Order No. 16. By Major E Beckwith M.C. Comdg 86th Company Machine Gun Corps. | 23/10/1916 | 23/10/1916 |
| Operation(al) Order(s) | In Continuation of Operation Order No. 16 | 23/10/1916 | 23/10/1916 |
| Miscellaneous | 86th Bde. Machine Gun Co. Operation Order. | | |
| Operation(al) Order(s) | Operation Order No. 16 Major & Beckwith Comdg. 86th Company Machine Gun Corps. | 23/10/1916 | 23/10/1916 |
| Miscellaneous | Operation Order By Major. A. Morris Commanding 88th Machine Gun Company 24th October 1916 | 24/10/1916 | 24/10/1916 |
| Heading | 29th Division. 86th Infantry Brigade. 86th Brigade. Machine Gun Company November 1916 | | |
| Heading | War Diary of the 86th Company Machine Gun Corps Volume IX. from 1st November 1916 to 30th November 1916. Vol 10 | | |
| War Diary | Corbie. | 01/11/1916 | 24/11/1916 |
| War Diary | Guillemont | 27/11/1916 | 30/11/1916 |
| Heading | 29th Division. 86th Infantry Brigade. 86th Brigade Machine Gun Company December 1916 | | |
| Heading | War Diary of 86th Company Machine Gun Corps from December 1st to December 31st 1916. Volume.10. Vol XI | | |
| War Diary | Guillemont | 01/12/1916 | 10/12/1916 |
| War Diary | Meaulte | 11/12/1916 | 19/12/1916 |
| War Diary | Ailly-Sur-Somme. | 20/12/1916 | 31/12/1916 |
| Heading | War Diary of 86th Company Machine Gun Corps from 1st January 1917 to 31st January 1917 (Volume XI). Vol 12 | | |
| War Diary | Ailly-Sur-Somme. | 01/01/1917 | 10/01/1917 |
| War Diary | Crouy | 11/01/1917 | 11/01/1917 |
| War Diary | Corbie. | 13/01/1917 | 13/01/1917 |
| War Diary | Treux. | 15/01/1917 | 15/01/1917 |
| War Diary | Guillemont. | 17/01/1917 | 23/01/1917 |
| War Diary | Mansell. | 25/01/1917 | 25/01/1917 |
| War Diary | Morval. | 26/01/1917 | 31/01/1917 |
| War Diary | Guillemont. | 31/01/1917 | 31/01/1917 |
| Miscellaneous | Machine Gun Instruction. | | |
| Map | | | |
| Heading | War Diary of 86th Company Machine Gun Corps from 1st February 1917 to 28th February 1917. Volume. XII. Vol.13 | | |
| War Diary | Guillemont | 01/02/1917 | 07/02/1917 |
| War Diary | Bussy by Daours. | 08/02/1917 | 12/02/1917 |
| War Diary | Bussy-Les-Daours | 13/02/1917 | 20/02/1917 |
| War Diary | Haiewood. | 21/02/1917 | 26/02/1917 |
| War Diary | Sailly Saillisel | 27/02/1917 | 28/02/1917 |
| Heading | War Diary of 86th Company Machine Gun Corps from 1st March 1917 to 31st March 1917. Volume. XIII. Vol.13 | | |
| War Diary | Haie Wood. | 01/03/1917 | 03/03/1917 |

| | | | |
|---|---|---|---|
| War Diary | Wedge Wood. | 04/03/1917 | 04/03/1917 |
| War Diary | Treux. | 05/03/1917 | 20/03/1917 |
| War Diary | Allery. | 21/03/1917 | 29/03/1917 |
| War Diary | Yzeux. | 30/03/1917 | 30/03/1917 |
| War Diary | Halloy. | 31/03/1917 | 31/03/1917 |
| Heading | War Diary of 86th Company, Machine Gun Corps. Volume.XIV. from 1st April 1917 to 30th April 1917. Vol.14 | | |
| War Diary | Halloy. | 01/04/1917 | 01/04/1917 |
| War Diary | Gezaincourt. | 02/04/1917 | 05/04/1917 |
| War Diary | Oppy. | 06/04/1917 | 07/04/1917 |
| War Diary | Warluzel | 08/04/1917 | 10/04/1917 |
| War Diary | Simencourt | 11/04/1917 | 12/04/1917 |
| War Diary | Arras. | 13/04/1917 | 13/04/1917 |
| War Diary | Tilloy. | 13/04/1917 | 14/04/1917 |
| War Diary | Feuchy | 15/04/1917 | 15/04/1917 |
| War Diary | Monchy-La-Preux | 16/04/1917 | 21/04/1917 |
| War Diary | Monchy-Le-Preux | 21/04/1917 | 21/04/1917 |
| War Diary | Arras. | 25/04/1917 | 25/04/1917 |
| War Diary | Bernville. | 26/04/1917 | 26/04/1917 |
| War Diary | Wanquentin | 27/04/1917 | 27/04/1917 |
| War Diary | Souastre. | 28/04/1917 | 30/04/1917 |
| Map | | | |
| Map | Map No. 3. Scale 1:10,000 Tops Section | | |
| Heading | War Diary of 86th Company Machine Gun Corps from 1st May 1917 to 31st May 1917. Volume. XV. Vol. 15 | | |
| War Diary | Souastre. | 01/05/1917 | 01/05/1917 |
| War Diary | Gouy-En-Artois. | 02/05/1917 | 02/05/1917 |
| War Diary | Arras. | 03/05/1917 | 11/05/1917 |
| War Diary | Dainville. | 12/05/1917 | 15/05/1917 |
| War Diary | Arras. | 16/05/1917 | 20/05/1917 |
| War Diary | Monchy. | 21/05/1917 | 30/05/1917 |
| Operation(al) Order(s) | 86th Brigade Order No. 139 | | |
| Operation(al) Order(s) | 29th Divisional Machine Gun Scheme issued in conjunction with 29th Division Order No. 121. dated 17th May 1917 | 17/05/1917 | 17/05/1917 |
| Operation(al) Order(s) | Appendix to 29th Division Order No. 121 | | |
| Map | Artillery Barrage Map. | | |
| Map | Trench Map. 86th Machine Gun Company. Scale-1:10,000 | | |
| Operation(al) Order(s) | 86th Machine Gun Company Operation Order No. 15. by Major E. Beckwith M.C. | 27/05/1917 | 27/05/1917 |
| Miscellaneous | Machine Gun Operation of 86th Machine Gun Company by Major E. Beckwith M.C. | 01/06/1917 | 01/06/1917 |
| Map | | | |
| Heading | War Diary of the 86th Coy. Machine Gun Corps for the period. 1st June 1917 to 30th June 1917. Volume XVI. Vol.16 | | |
| War Diary | Arras. | 01/06/1917 | 02/06/1917 |
| War Diary | Bernville. | 03/06/1917 | 03/06/1917 |
| War Diary | St Hilaire. | 04/06/1917 | 17/06/1917 |
| War Diary | Halloy. | 18/06/1917 | 26/06/1917 |
| War Diary | Haandeket. | 27/06/1917 | 30/06/1917 |
| Heading | War Diary of 86th Company. Machine Gun Corps. from 1st July 1917 to 31st July 1917. Volume. XVII. Vol.17 | | |
| War Diary | Handekot | 01/07/1916 | 04/07/1916 |

| | | | |
|---|---|---|---|
| War Diary | Dragon Camp. | 05/07/1917 | 12/07/1917 |
| War Diary | In The Line. | 13/07/1917 | 20/07/1917 |
| War Diary | Corps Staging Area No. 2 | 21/07/1917 | 31/07/1917 |
| Heading | War Diary. Of the 86th Company-Machine Gun Corps for the period. from 1st August 1917 to 31st August 1917. Volume.18 | | |
| War Diary | Corps Staging Area No. 2 | 01/08/1917 | 06/08/1917 |
| War Diary | No. 16. Camp. | 07/08/1917 | 07/08/1917 |
| War Diary | Forest Area. | 08/08/1917 | 08/08/1917 |
| War Diary | In The Line. | 09/08/1917 | 24/08/1917 |
| War Diary | Forest Area. | 25/08/1917 | 26/08/1917 |
| War Diary | Front Camp | 27/08/1917 | 31/08/1917 |
| Miscellaneous | Operation Orders by Captain J.P. Roberts Commanding 86th Company Machine Gun Corps. | | |
| Miscellaneous | Appendix A. 29th Division M.G. Barrage Instructions. | | |
| Operation(al) Order(s) | Operation Orders No. 2 | | |
| Heading | War Diary of the 86th Company Machine Gun Corps for the period from 1st September 1917 to 30th September 1917 Volume XIX. Vol.19 | | |
| War Diary | Point Camp. | 01/09/1917 | 16/09/1917 |
| War Diary | Herzeele | 17/09/1917 | 19/09/1917 |
| War Diary | Point Camp. | 20/09/1917 | 20/09/1917 |
| War Diary | Wellington Camp. (In reserve). | 21/09/1917 | 27/09/1917 |
| War Diary | Wellington Camp. | 28/09/1917 | 30/09/1917 |
| Heading | War Diary of the 86th Company-Machine Gun Corps for the period from 1st October 1917 to 31st October 1917. Volume XX. Vol.20 | | |
| War Diary | Wellington Camp. | 01/10/1917 | 06/10/1917 |
| War Diary | Dulwich Camp. | 07/10/1917 | 08/10/1917 |
| War Diary | In The Line. | 09/10/1917 | 10/10/1917 |
| War Diary | Proven. | 11/10/1917 | 15/10/1917 |
| War Diary | Parana Camp. | 16/10/1917 | 17/10/1917 |
| War Diary | Blairville. | 18/10/1917 | 31/10/1917 |
| Operation(al) Order(s) | Operation Order No. 6. By Captain J.P. Row Commanding 86th Company Machine Gun Corps. | 02/10/1917 | 02/10/1917 |
| Operation(al) Order(s) | 86th Machine Gun Company Operation Order No. 7 | | |
| Miscellaneous | Barrage-Instructions. | | |
| War Diary | Blairville Camp No 2 | 01/11/1917 | 17/11/1917 |
| War Diary | Haut-Allaine. | 18/11/1917 | 19/11/1917 |
| War Diary | Equancourt | 20/11/1917 | 20/11/1917 |
| War Diary | Villiers Pluich | 21/11/1917 | 21/11/1917 |
| War Diary | Marcoing. | 22/11/1917 | 23/11/1917 |
| War Diary | Masnieres | 24/11/1917 | 30/11/1917 |
| Miscellaneous | Brigade Major 86th Bde. | 21/12/1917 | 21/12/1917 |
| War Diary | In The Line | 01/12/1917 | 02/12/1917 |
| War Diary | Ribecourt | 03/12/1917 | 03/12/1917 |
| War Diary | Havringcourt Wood | 04/12/1917 | 04/12/1917 |
| War Diary | Finns | 05/12/1917 | 05/12/1917 |
| War Diary | Petit Houvin | 06/12/1917 | 06/12/1917 |
| War Diary | Magnicourt | 07/12/1917 | 16/12/1917 |
| War Diary | Blangerval | 17/12/1917 | 17/12/1917 |
| War Diary | Wamin | 18/12/1917 | 18/12/1917 |
| War Diary | Sehen | 19/12/1917 | 03/01/1918 |
| War Diary | Setques | 04/01/1918 | 16/01/1918 |
| War Diary | Brandhoek | 17/01/1918 | 17/01/1918 |
| War Diary | Junction Camp | 18/01/1918 | 20/01/1918 |

| War Diary | In The Line. | 21/01/1918 | 28/01/1918 |
| War Diary | Brandhoek. | 29/01/1918 | 31/01/1918 |

WO 95/23021 6

29TH DIVISION
86TH INFY BDE

86TH COY. MACHINE GUN CORPS

FEB 1916 - ~~FEB~~ 1918
JAN

29th Division.
86th Infntry Brigade.

ARRIVED MARSEILLES FROM EGYPT 26th March 1916.

86th BRIGADE

MACHINE GUN COMPANY

27th FEBRUARY to 30th APRIL

1 9 1 6

# 86th Brigade Machine Gun Co.

## WAR DIARY or INTELLIGENCE SUMMARY

Army Form C. 2118.

| Place | Date | Hour | Summary of Events and Information | Remarks and references to Appendices |
|---|---|---|---|---|
| SUEZ | 1916 27th Feby | | The 86th Brigade Machine Gun Company was formed. The nucleus of the Company was formed from the existing Machine Gun Sections of the Battalions in the 86th Brigade. The following were the Officers on formation:— Captain E. Beckwith 2nd Bn Royal Fusiliers Lieutenants K.J. McAlpin " U.J. Maray " H.V. Wilkinson " J.B. Stevenson 1st Bn Lancashire Fusiliers " J.O. Eaton " " " " D.J.P. Duffy " " " " M. Milne 1st Bn. Roy. Munster Fusiliers " 14th D.L.I. (atta 1st R Dublin Fus") " A. Byrne 1st Bn R. Dublin Fusiliers Embarked at Port Suez on H.M.T. Lake Manitoba for France (B.E.F.) | |
| Suez | 16th March | | " | |
| | 21st | | " | |
| Marseilles | 26th March | | Arrived Marseilles remained on board till following day. | |

Army Form C. 2118.

# WAR DIARY
## or
## INTELLIGENCE SUMMARY.
*(Erase heading not required.)*

Instructions regarding War Diaries and Intelligence Summaries are contained in F. S. Regs., Part II. and the Staff Manual respectively. Title pages will be prepared in manuscript.

| Place | Date | Hour | Summary of Events and Information | Remarks and references to Appendices |
|---|---|---|---|---|
| | 1916 | | | |
| Marseilles | 27th March | | Entrained at 1400 for PONT REMY a distance of 9 miles | |
| PONT REMY | 29th March | | Arrived at PONT REMY then proceed by March Route to Billets at La PLOUY | |
| La PLOUY | 31st March | | moved to Beauval by march route and Billetted | |

# WAR DIARY
## or
## INTELLIGENCE SUMMARY.
*(Erase heading not required.)*

Army Form C. 2118.

| Place | Date | Hour | Summary of Events and Information | Remarks and references to Appendices |
|---|---|---|---|---|
| | 1916 | | | |
| BEAUVAL | 1st April | | The Company remained in Billets. The Equipping of the Company Transport was practically completed with the exception of Riding Horses for Section Officers. | |
| BEAUVAL | 2nd April | | Captain E. Beckwith (O.C. Co.) went on leave to England. Lieut. A.F. St.Albin assumed temporary command of the Company. | |
| BEAUVAL | 3rd April | | Lieut. O.J.Q. Duffy met with accident whilst riding his horse. He was removed to Kashalty Clearing Station. | |
| BEAUVAL | 4th April | | The Company proceeded by march route to Billets at ACHIEUX. | |
| ACHIEUX | 5th April | | 4 Guns W.S.E. mounted for Anti-Aircraft purposes. | |
| " | 9th April | | Lieut Wilkinson rejoined from leave | |
| " | 13th April | | Marched to MAILLEY MAILLET to relieve 87th Machine Gun Company in the Trenches as follows:— | |
| MAILLEY MAILLET | 13th April | | No.1 Section took over Auchion VILLERS Guns under Lieut F. Dandy. This later to WHITE CITY as extreme left of Brigade Line. | |
| | | | No.2 Section under Lieut WHITE CITY on extreme left of Brigade Line | |
| | | | No.4 Section under Lieut MILNE and BYRNE took over KNIGHTSBRIDGE BARRACKS | |

# WAR DIARY
## INTELLIGENCE SUMMARY.
*(Erase heading not required.)*

Army Form C. 2118.

Instructions regarding War Diaries and Intelligence Summaries are contained in F. S. Regs., Part II. and the Staff Manual respectively. Title pages will be prepared in manuscript.

| Place | Date | Hour | Summary of Events and Information | Remarks and references to Appendices |
|---|---|---|---|---|
| | 1916 | | | |
| MAILLY MAILLET | 13th April | | On 13th night 87th Brigade Rel., No3 remained in Reserve at MAILLY | |
| | 14th April | | Captain E. Beckwith rejoined from England and assumed Command of Company | |
| | 15th April | | Captain Beckwith and Lieut McAlpin accompanied Brigadier General Williams DSO on a tour of inspection of the 87th Brigade front line | |
| | 16th April | | Offr. Comdg. Company inspected existing machine gun positions and decided on several more suitable positions | |
| | 20th April | | 87th Machine Gun Company relieves KNIGHTSBRIDGE BARRACKS. 3 Gun Positions. No 4 Section on being relieved by 87th returned to Billets at MAILLEY MAILLET.<br>No1 Section moved into new gun positions at CARDIFF TRENCH and NEWTOWNARDS.<br>No3 took over the AUCHION VILLERS Sector | |
| | 21st April | | Officer Comdg. Company allotted 2 new gun Posts one at the BOWERY and one at YOUNG STREET to strengthen sub front line. A fine MaRing in all 7 guns in 1st line and 4 guns in 2nd line. the MaRing nights continued very heavy. The whole of the night was a perfect deluge. MaRing work in the trenches extremely difficult | |

**WAR DIARY**
or
**INTELLIGENCE SUMMARY.**
*(Erase heading not required.)*

Army Form C. 2118.

| Place | Date | Hour | Summary of Events and Information | Remarks and references to Appendices |
|---|---|---|---|---|
| MAILLEY MAILLET | 1916 19/6 22nd April | | Officer commanding Company accompanied Divisional Staff Officer round the Machine Gun positions who approved his approval of the sites selected. | |
| | 23rd April | | 6th Bde Company moved the Transport lines and billets of the Bn. Or ACHEUX. No 5 Section under Lieut. Wilkinson moved from AUCHONVILLERS to WHITE CITY to relieve No 2 Section under Lieut. Later who returned with his section to MAILLEY MAILLET for a rest. No 4 Section under LIEUT. MILNE moved out of billets to AUCHONVILLERS in relief of No 3 section. The weather considerably improved during the day rain appearing during the mid-day. | |
| | 28th April | | 87th Brigade relieved 86th Brigade in firing line. 86th Brigade Machine gun Coy attached to 87th Brigade for duty. No guns were not relieved from positions. | |
| | 29th April | | Officer Commanding Company attended Conference at Brigade H.Q. | |

**Army Form C. 2118.**

# WAR DIARY
## or
## INTELLIGENCE SUMMARY.
*(Erase heading not required.)*

Instructions regarding War Diaries and Intelligence Summaries are contained in F. S. Regs., Part II. and the Staff Manual respectively. Title pages will be prepared in manuscript.

| Place | Date | Hour | Summary of Events and Information | Remarks and references to Appendices |
|---|---|---|---|---|
| | 1916 | | | |
| Mailley Maillet | 29th April | | to discuss operation for night of 29th-30th April. Lieut. Stevenson proceeded to England on leave also Company Sergeant Major. | |
| | | | Night of 29-30th we got 10 guns into position. Operation coming off during night. Raid into the German trenches successfully. Two (?) casualties from own company Shrapnel. Spluster Cpl. Lroll, Pte. Phillipson & Pte. Newnham all wounded. | |
| | 30th April | | 2 Lectures under Lieut. S.O. & Co returned wind. S.O. Bath at the CARDIFF TRENCH sector. The weather for the past week has been good. The trenches now being in a fairly condition. | |

Edward DeWink Captain.
Comdg. 86th Brigade Machine Gun Company
30th April 1916.

29

86 Bde M G Coy

Vol I
 II
 III

29th Division.
86th Infantry Brigade.

86th BRIGADE

MACHINE GUN COMPANY

M A Y 1 9 1 6

O a h
G.H.Q
3rd Echelon

1st June 1916

Herewith original copy of
War Diary of 86th Brigade Machine
Gun Company for Week of May
1916.

[signature] Captain
Comdg. 86th Brigade Machine Gun Co.

Army Form C. 2118.

86th Brigade Machine Gun Co.

WAR DIARY
or
INTELLIGENCE SUMMARY.

Instructions regarding War Diaries and Intelligence Summaries are contained in F.S. Regs., Part II. and the Staff Manual respectively. Title pages will be prepared in manuscript.

(Erase heading not required.)

| Place | Date | Hour | Summary of Events and Information | Remarks and references to Appendices |
|---|---|---|---|---|
| | 1916 | | | |
| MAILLEY MAILLET | 1ST MAY | | Lieut P.A. BYRNE proceeded on leave to England. As a result of the bombardment on the night of 29/30 BEAUMONT SAP was considerably knocked about and a machine gun emplacement destroyed. At about 2030 a party of the enemy suddenly rushed up to our wire on the R. of N°2 Sap and threw 12 bombs into our wire. Our machine guns fired on the party who ran away. Hostile artillery then opened up a violent bombardment. This lasted 15 to 20 minutes when the fire was raised. A patrol of the S.W. BORDERS reported enemy busy repairing their wire. Machine guns were directed at the wire and bursts continued. | |
| | 2nd MAY | | Shells fell in vicinity of AUCHIONVILLERS guns, no damage done to emplacements or guns, the shells appeared to have two explosions with about a seconds interval. Pigeons were observed to fly from behind our lines into Enemy's lines. | |

# WAR DIARY
## or
## INTELLIGENCE SUMMARY

| Place | Date | Hour | Summary of Events and Information | Remarks and references to Appendices |
|---|---|---|---|---|
| MAILLY MAILLET | 1916 | | | |
| | 30 May | | Lance Corporal Tomlinson went on leave to England. Enemy trench mortars, guns and artillery very quiet during the night. A burst was put on 2 flares were sent up. The enemy sent out a WHITE FLASH over the front trench at K 35 A 39 B 5 testing the lights. | |
| | 1st May | | KUT EL AMARA has been taken, 8000 prisoners. Trenches at CARDIFF STREET and BUT AVENUE were shelled 15pm heavily during the morning, but no damage was done to the emplacements. A rifle of musketry from our lines at JACOB'S LADDER, and from a large working party on SUNKEN ROAD and guns was turned on the road. | |
| | 5th May | | In AUCHONVILLERS a considerable number of shells were sent over by the enemy during the morning no damage was done. A new emplacement was started in ESSEX STREET to replace one CARDIFF TRENCH which has on the corner for a good amount of shelling. | |

# WAR DIARY
## or
## INTELLIGENCE SUMMARY.

*(Erase heading not required.)*

Army Form C. 2118.

| Place | Date | Hour | Summary of Events and Information | Remarks and references to Appendices |
|---|---|---|---|---|
| MAILLEY MAILLET | 1916 6th May | | Hostile artillery was more active than usual, the front line and supporting line were shelled persistently. Machine guns were active against our Aircraft. At midnight our Machine guns opened fire in conjunction with our Artillery. Our new Emplacement at ESSEX STREET was connected with main trench by a narrow communication trench being dug during the night. | |
| — | 7th May | | During the day the enemy shelled the MARY REDAN and E.6 CONSTITUTIONAL HILL and filled in the trenches to a considerable extent. Towards dusk things quieted; but at 2300 the enemy fired heavy shells over our lines. Our Artillery replied and all was quiet again about 0045. PILK STREET gun fired on enemy working party in front line about 1800 and again on enemy wire at 2400. 2/Lt. NOONAN went on leave to England. AUCHIONVILLERS came in for some shelling during afternoon and evening no damage done. | |
| — | 8th May | | A new kind of Aeroplane was observed flying over our | |

**Army Form C. 2118.**

# WAR DIARY
## or
## INTELLIGENCE SUMMARY.
*(Erase heading not required.)*

Instructions regarding War Diaries and Intelligence Summaries are contained in F. S. Regs., Part II. and the Staff Manual respectively. Title pages will be prepared in manuscript.

| Place | Date | Hour | Summary of Events and Information | Remarks and references to Appendices |
|---|---|---|---|---|
| MAILLY MAILLET | 1916 8th May | | Continued:- the N. sector of our lines. LIEUT. J. STEVENSON returned off leave from England. No 2 Section under Lieut CREASEY relieved No 1 SECTION at AUCHIONVILLIERS. No 1 Section under Lieut HARDY relieved No 4 Section at WHITE CITY and No 3 Section from MAILLEY MAILLET under Lieut WILKINSON relieved No 2 Section at 2nd AVENUE | |
| " | 9th May | | Enemy artillery fairly Quiet, their chief target being a new trench at AUCHIONVILLIERS. Machine Gunners also Quiet. It is probable that reliefs were taking place. There was very little for our Guns to fire at. Lieut McALPINE and Private O'BRIEN proceed on leave to England. The following men were posted to the Company from its machine Gun Base ETAPES No 8972 Pte WOOD F. 40091 Pte TIFFIN A. 11915  Pte WHITWORTH C. 9403  O'REILLY R | |

# WAR DIARY
## or
## INTELLIGENCE SUMMARY.
*(Erase heading not required.)*

Army Form C. 2118.

| Place | Date | Hour | Summary of Events and Information | Remarks and references to Appendices |
|---|---|---|---|---|
| MAILLY MAILLET | 1916 10th May | | At LIMERICK JUNCTION a H.E. shell dropped killing one man and injuring 2 men of the 87th M.G. Co. no damage to our own men. A Patrol on our R. Sector reports that the enemy were wiring, our machine guns opened fire on the position and the party must have retired no further work was heard observed near our Auchionvillers Guns report that the uniform of the enemy opposite is cleaner & smarter than formerly. This suggested that this may mean that reliefs have been recently taken place as reported yesterday 10th. | ER |
| — | 11th May | | at about 2130 four shells (two failing to explode) were fired at our BOWERY GUN position but no damage was. A patrol reports that the enemy were wiring at HAWTHORNE REDOUBT & AVENUE gun was turned on the REDOUBT and the noise ceased. A very bright white flare went up behind BEAUMONT HAMEL, this was followed by a burst of SHRAPNEL. | |

Army Form C. 2118.

# WAR DIARY
## or
## INTELLIGENCE SUMMARY.
(Erase heading not required.)

Instructions regarding War Diaries and Intelligence Summaries are contained in F. S. Regs., Part II. and the Staff Manual respectively. Title pages will be prepared in manuscript.

| Place | Date | Hour | Summary of Events and Information | Remarks and references to Appendices |
|---|---|---|---|---|
| MAILLY MAILLET | 12th May | 10.16 | The trenches N. of our NEW BEAUMONT ROAD Sap were shelled at various points between 0800 and 0900. King Street in front of 4th AVENUE was enfiladed. Fourteen heavy shells were fired at the BOWERY between 1000 and 1100 the majority falling short, no damage was done to any of our Gun positions. Enemy Machine Guns traversed our front line. We replied with VICKERS and LEWIS Gun fire at Q10.d 80.75 from which the machine gun fire was suspected to come. A new Gun Emplacement was completed and occupied to replace exposed gun position at CARDIFF TRENCH. at ESSEX STREET | |
| | 13th May | | The Enemy was on the whole quiet in our Sector. The BOWERY was shelled but no damage done to Emplacements. A small patrol left our lines to examine Saps in enemy line. After proceeding short distance they sighted hostile patrol about 25 strong some distance away. Our patrol retired and our Machine Guns fired on enemy patrol which also retired. | |

# WAR DIARY
## or
## INTELLIGENCE SUMMARY.
(Erase heading not required.)

Army Form C. 2118.

| Place | Date | Hour | Summary of Events and Information | Remarks and references to Appendices |
|---|---|---|---|---|
| MAILLY MAILLET | 1916 14th May | | The weather has been very uncertain during latter part of the week accompanied by heavy rain, making movement work in the trenches difficult. Strength of Company stands at 9 officers 1 W.O. and 139 other ranks. No 4 Section under Lieut BYRNE relieved No 2 section at AUCHONVILLERS. No 2 section returning to MAILLY MAILLET Lieut CREASEY took over 2nd AVENUE guns. Lieut LATER and C.Q.M.S. SULLIVAN proceeded on leave to England last night 14th | |
| — | 15th May | | Lieut D.J.P. DUFFY rejoined the Company from Base. ETAPES. Artillery operations were much below normal. The enemy shelled our line at Q.4. 7/8 doing no damage. Considerable artillery and machine gun activity was heard about 22.45 on our right at a distance of 2-3 miles Very few flares from were seen by Enemy last two or three nights. | |

Army Form C. 2118.

# WAR DIARY
## or
## INTELLIGENCE SUMMARY.
*(Erase heading not required.)*

| Place | Date | Hour | Summary of Events and Information | Remarks and references to Appendices |
|---|---|---|---|---|
| MAILLEY MAILLET | 1916 16th May | | Two new Gun sites were started in the 4th Avenue in connection with a Scheme for future Operations and two sites at the BOWERY were Completed. A demonstration of Machine Guns (VICKERS and LEWIS) was carried out in accordance with attached Operation Order. At 0 o'clock two Red flares were sent up and on the bursting of the 2nd flare all Machine guns opened fired on "NO MANS LAND", Enemy's Front line and Wire. At 0010 two Red flares was again sent up and fire ceased on bursting of 2nd flare. Within a few seconds of our opening fire the enemy turned on traversing fire with their M/guns (about 4 guns) on cessation of our fire at 0010 the Enemy sent over 8 small shells in vicinity of Q.10-10.15 | |
| | 17th May | | The enemy fired a few shells into MAILLEY MAILLET about 1530. | |

# WAR DIARY
## or
## INTELLIGENCE SUMMARY.

Army Form C. 2118.

| Place | Date | Hour | Summary of Events and Information | Remarks and references to Appendices |
|---|---|---|---|---|
| MAILLEY MAILLET | 1916 18th May | | Lieut. McAlpin returned to duty from England. No 3 Section under Lieut McAlpin took over AUCHIONVILLER SECTOR. No 4 Section under Lieut BYRNE took over 2nd AVENUE SECTOR No 3 under Lieuts Stevenson and Duffy took WHITE CITY Sector. No 1 Section returning to MAILLEY MAILLET. The enemy chiefly confined their shelling at Aeroplanes during the day. The night was comparatively Quiet. Shells were observed to drop on the Road at Q.14 during the morning, a large proportion of which did not explode. The following N.C.O. men of the Company were mentioned in Genl. Sir Iam Hamilton's despatch of Dec 11th 1915. "London Gazette d/Jan 28th 1916 2733 Sergeant Duffy(A) (now C.S.Major) M.G. CORPS. no 30898 10085 Lance Corporal J. O'Brien 8961 Sergeant D McCormack | |

# WAR DIARY or INTELLIGENCE SUMMARY

Army Form C. 2118.

| Place | Date | Hour | Summary of Events and Information | Remarks and references to Appendices |
|---|---|---|---|---|
| MAILLY MAILLET | 19/5/16 | | A new Gun pit was started at a place 80'N of ONE TREE. this position is purely defensive. At 0215 the enemy sent over about 30 rounds of Shrapnel over the trenches N.B. N.E.N. BEAUMONT ROAD we not replied. At 1630 our Guns fired on an enemy working party in trench Q.6.c.60-45 which dispersed the party. An Officer and one man (1st Lancs Fus.) went out through Sap 7 Q.48/9 at 2045 to the Sunken road. this party sent back a guide to take a party of 16th Middlesex to bring body of a German soldier Officer killed the previous night | |
| | 20/5/16 | | The enemy fired Shrapnel shells on the transport approach W. of White City. A few heavy shells were fired into S.E. of MAILLY MAILLET at 2050. At midday about 30 shells were fired into the BROADWAY, 3 men of a working party being wounded. During the day a notice board appeared in the enemy's lines bearing the following | |

# WAR DIARY
or
## INTELLIGENCE SUMMARY.
(Erase heading not required.)

| Place | Date | Hour | Summary of Events and Information | Remarks and references to Appendices |
|---|---|---|---|---|
| | 1916 | | Continued — | |
| MAILLY | 20th May | | Lieut. UREN dead and buried what about VISHOF LEHMANN? | |
| MAILLY | | | Also refers to the Junior officer referred to on 19th. A board has been put up on our front line to-day informing the enemy that LEHMANN is dead, buried and grave marked. | |
| | | | At 9.40 pm Sentries reported a hostile aeroplane over our line. It was pursued by two of our aeroplanes and brought down in flames beyond THIEPVAL WOOD. | |
| | | | A small Red Balloon fell in our lines. It appeared to come from the direction of GRANDCOURT and was visible for a long way. Attached to it were two copies of the "Continental Times" containing lying and lurid reports of the recent revolt in Ireland. Some headings were "Stories taken from leading British newspapers", "Shooting men and women for wearing of the Green", "Slaughtering little children" | |

**Army Form C. 2118.**

# WAR DIARY
## or
## INTELLIGENCE SUMMARY.
(Erase heading not required.)

Instructions regarding War Diaries and Intelligence Summaries are contained in F.S. Regs., Part II. and the Staff Manual respectively. Title pages will be prepared in manuscript.

| Place | Date | Hour | Summary of Events and Information | Remarks and references to Appendices |
|---|---|---|---|---|
| MAILLY MAILLET | 1916 20th May | | continued:— "Why I went to Germany" by Jn. Roger Casement. There was also a Cartoon depicting "John Bull" Scourging ERIN tied to a post. | |
| | 21st May | | The enemy sent over about 20 rounds of Shrapnel & H.E. over the front line N. of New BEAUMONT Rd. This was preceded by Two Red flares. In reply our Artillery put about 12 rounds into enemy front line. Working parties in the Communication trenches in Area Q.10.c. were fired upon, no casualties. | |
| | 22nd May | | The Enemy's trench mortors showed some activity in the Auchonvillers sector. Also machine guns on the same place. The Enemy sent up flares which gave no warning of their approach either by sound or flash previous to bursting into light. A Whistle blast was used by a German sentry as a signal for Machine Gun fire to be opened. | |
| | 23rd May | | about 1600 the enemy sent shells on the road near Q.3.B.5-4 | |

# WAR DIARY
## or
## INTELLIGENCE SUMMARY.
*(Erase heading not required.)*

Army Form C. 2118.

| Place | Date | Hour | Summary of Events and Information | Remarks and references to Appendices |
|---|---|---|---|---|
| MAILLY MAILLET | 1916 23rd May | | the shells passing over WHITE CITY with a following wind. Seven shells were fired on AUCHIONVILLERS about 1100 and four more at 1545. | |
| | 24th May | | The enemy have been improving their defences at various points notably in front of and behind BEAUMONT HAMEL. The Village of BEAUMONT was shelled for about an hour with shrapnel and H.E. at 7.30pm the enemy fired a burst of shrapnel over the NEW BEAUMONT ROAD. Several Officers patrols went out in the AUCHIONVILLERS Sector without casualty. | |
| | 25th May | | No 2 Section under Lieut McALPIN took over WHITE CITY from No 3 Section who returned to MAILLY MAILLET. No 1 Section took over AUCHIONVILLERS | |
| | 26th May | | The enemy sent some shrapnel and 12 H.E. into AUCHIONVILLERS 2nd Avenue, P.O.R.R and firing line have been drawn with Range O | |

# WAR DIARY
## or
## INTELLIGENCE SUMMARY.
(Erase heading not required.)

Army Form C. 2118.

| Place | Date | Hour | Summary of Events and Information | Remarks and references to Appendices |
|---|---|---|---|---|
| | 19/6 | | | |
| MAILLET | 27th May | | In the AUCHONVILLERS sector some particularly heavy H.E. was fired at our line, no damage was done. Patrols went out from our sector to examine enemy's wire, which they found strong, thick and well erected. The enemy fire was directed on our trenches, some H.E. came over | |
| MAILLET | 28th May | | but no damage was done. A few 5.9 c.m. shells fell in Orchard Q.13.B. (MAILLEY) causing slight casualties to a working party. | |
| | 29th May | | Our Artillery was more active than usual registering on the enemy's trenches in the HAWTHORNE REDOUBT and BEAUMONT HAMEL. A good deal of damage was done to the enemy wire opposite Q.10.6 as a result of the Counter Bombardment between 11.30 p.m. and 12.30 a.m. Some damage was done to our trenches on the left of the AUCHONVILLERS sector and we suffered some casualties. Our machine guns were very active on the night 29/30th. | |

**Army Form C. 2118.**

# WAR DIARY
## or
## INTELLIGENCE SUMMARY.
(Erase heading not required.)

Instructions regarding War Diaries and Intelligence Summaries are contained in F. S. Regs., Part II. and the Staff Manual respectively. Title pages will be prepared in manuscript.

| Place | Date | Hour | Summary of Events and Information | Remarks and references to Appendices |
|---|---|---|---|---|
| | 1916 | | | |
| MAILLEY | 29th May | | 88th Machine Gun Company. The whole of our Company was relieved in the line by the 88th Machine Gun Company. The relief was completed by 1300. The Company then proceeded by march route to billets at LOUVENCOURT. | |
| MAILLET | 30th May | | The Officer Comdg Co. accompanied the Brigadier General to ACHIEUX to view a section of the ground on a scale of 1/20 of the Enemy trenches laid down on the ground on a scale of 1/20 | |
| | 31st May | | The Officer Comdg Co. attended a Conference of Commanding Officers under the Presidency of the Brigadier General to discuss a scheme for Brigade operations for Training Purposes. The Brigadier General thanked the Commanding Officers for the excellent manner in which all ranks had worked whilst in the trenches & wished his thanks to be conveyed to the Men | |

Edward Rowith Captain
Comdg. 86th Brigade Machine Gun Company
LOUVENCOURT. 31st May 1916.

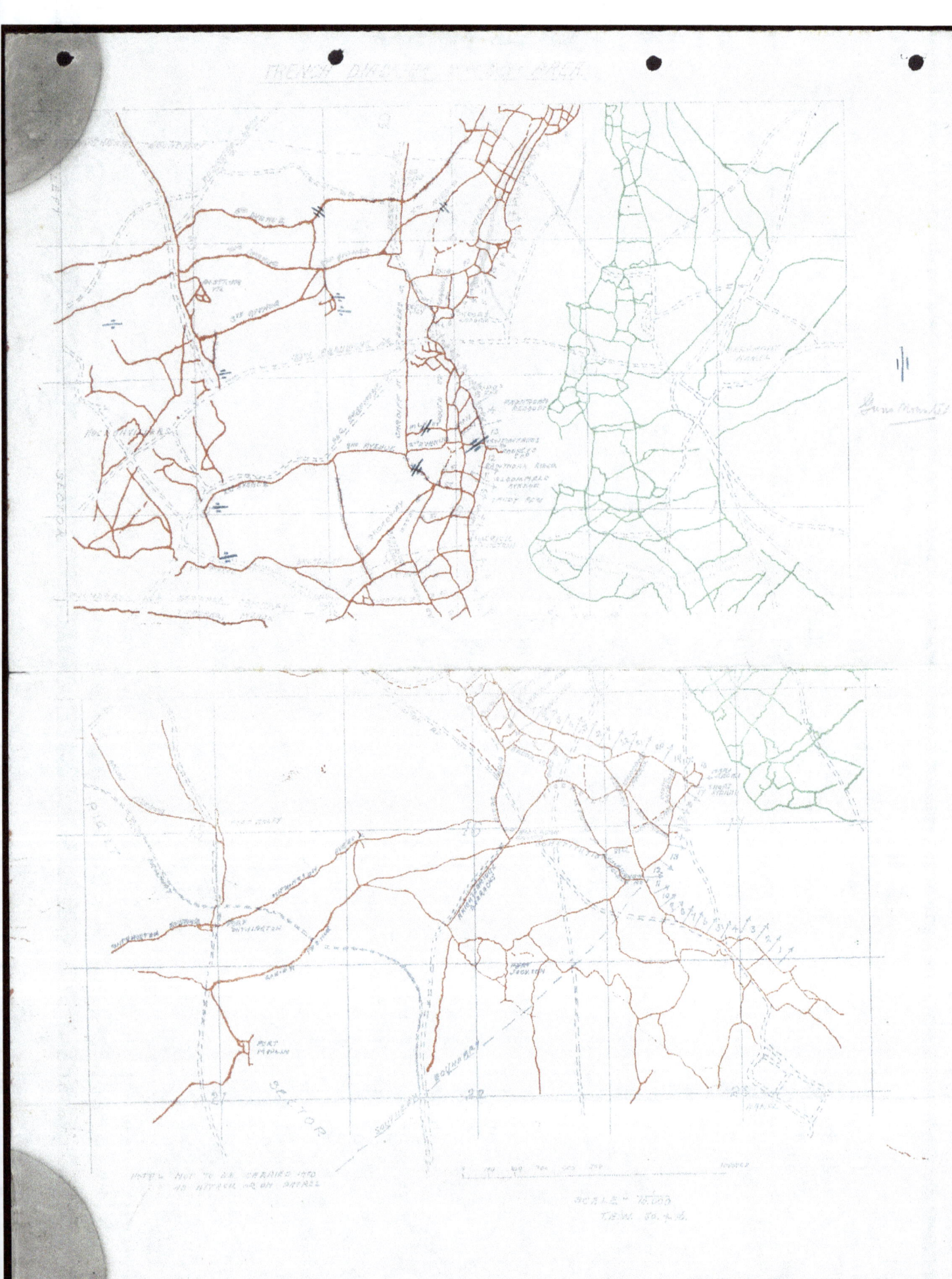

29th Division.

86th Infantry Brigade

-----

86th BRIGADE

MACHINE GUN COMPANY

JULY 1916

Appendices attached:-

Operation Orders.

Casualty List.

Army Form C. 2118.

86th Brigade Machine Gun Co. **WAR DIARY** or **INTELLIGENCE SUMMARY**

Vol 6

(Erase heading not required.)

| Place | Date | Hour | Summary of Events and Information | Remarks and references to Appendices |
|---|---|---|---|---|
| Auchonvillers | 1st July | 10/6 | In accordance with orders attached [?]. On the night of the 30th June 1916 the Company was situated as follows:- | |
| | | | In the Line:- 2guns at the Bowery under Lieut. J.F.B. Stevenson | |
| | | | 1 gun at Pick Street — " — M. Milne | |
| | | | 1 gun at Essex Street — " — } J.P. | |
| | | | 1 gun at Newfoundwards — " — } Lieut. Day. Duffy | |
| | | | 1 gun at "F" Street | |
| | | | 2 guns at MAILLEY MAILLET under Lieut. H.V. Wilkinson | |
| | | | 8 guns at Acheux together with Company Headquarters | |
| | | | At 2 A.M. the 30th these 8 guns and Headquarters moved into the line by the following Route:- Rotten Row | |
| | | | New Track | |
| | | | Broadway | |
| | | | 2nd Avenue | |
| | | | In accordance with attack instructions. Arriving in the line the guns were disposed of as follows:- 6 guns remained in position in line as above | |
| | | | 4 guns joined Royal Fusiliers | |
| | | | 3 guns — " — Lancashire Fusiliers | |
| | | | 2 guns — " — to King Street to reinforce Lancashire Fus. | |
| | | | 2 guns — " — to "F" Street to reinforce Royal Fusiliers | |

Army Form C. 118.

# WAR DIARY
## or
## INTELLIGENCE SUMMARY
(Erase heading not required.)

| Place | Date | Hour | Summary of Events and Information | Remarks and references to Appendices |
|---|---|---|---|---|
| AUCHON VILLERS | 1st July 1916 | | at 0015' all Gun teams reported they were in position ready for the assault. Equipment carried. Ration of S.A.A. Water dumps are shown on attached | |
| | | | Sketch and in Operation orders. | |
| | | | Strength of Company going into Action:— | |
| | | | 10 Officers. 1 M.O. | |
| | | | 139 O.R.s | |
| | | | Artillery Bombardment — enemy, was intermittently intense throughout the night immediately following the assault (0730) it became very intense sweeping our support trenches more heavily than the front line, with a view of preventing reinforcements coming up. This continued throughout the morning until about 1030 ## when it gradually became less and by 12 noon it had dwindled to desultory fire, replying only sharply when our own sent up heavier old Wing. Our Artillery, maintained throughout the night (30/6-1/7) a continuous steady fire on the enemy's 1st & 2nd systems of trenches at about 6 a.m. an intense Bombardment was commenced by the guns this continued up to true | |

**Army Form C. 2118.** (3)

# WAR DIARY
## or
## INTELLIGENCE SUMMARY
*(Erase heading not required.)*

| Place | Date | Hour | Summary of Events and Information | Remarks and references to Appendices |
|---|---|---|---|---|
| AUCHON- VILLERS | 1916 1st July | 6.45 a.m. | Of the assault when the Artillery lifted, in accordance the operation orders. The Bombardment continued intense until about 11.30 a.m. when it diminished somewhat at 7.20 a.m. however a matter heavy fire was again put on the German front line for 5 hours. At 0720 a mine was exploded under the HAWTHORNE Redoubt near Point Q. As soon as the debris had settled 4 machine guns under Lieut K.D McAlpin proceeded over to the N. Lip of the Crater. Arriving at this Guns 2 Guns were placed down front line of trenches running N. and 2 guns firing down trenches running S. These Guns were immediately followed by 2 Platoons of the 2nd Battalion Royal Fusiliers and a team of Stoke Gunners. Lieutenant K.D McAlpin reports that he could see the front trenches of the German trenches to the "N" that the trenches had been badly knocked in by our Artillery & that he was able to see Parties of the enemy from the lines upwards. He estimated that a | |

Army Form C. 2118.

# WAR DIARY
## or
## INTELLIGENCE SUMMARY
(Erase heading not required.)

| Place | Date | Hour | Summary of Events and Information | Remarks and references to Appendices |
|---|---|---|---|---|
| AUCHION-VILLERS | 1st July | | Assumed a cross out front and attempts to form up with the Royal Berks on the Right and the R/Dublin Fus agoor. Punctual at 06.30 or so the German wire & arrive up thro' Wicket by the Enemy M.Gun Gun fire. At 0950 the wheels but by Observer to be falling back or our front line infantry with Hun retaliating paper got back into the Sunken Road and thence into the through Sap 87. At about 09.15 or so the C.O. 2nd Lts Ind. Harmann two Runners went over. Very shortly after the Runners at 2 Party, men Serjt. Sap Errmon informed the C.O. that Lieut. S. also and a Boy wounded were also on out of His Turm and that Lieut Dun, Brennan & Lees also been wounded and one Runner killed by M.guns also stated that the Lancs. Inns. Irish Bde. under Lt. Stephens right and to the left with Lieuts. Kush, B.J. Fitzgerald, Turpin & the Surgd. Major of the line, arriving there found the two guns of the Up. rectors hin reting to by put out and their crew to be mounted on the parapet to shelter & work the two guns. Lon brought up the totally to Cross the Ayed Wood was held in the Sunken Road also sent Lt. E.P. Lowes a message telling |

# WAR DIARY or INTELLIGENCE SUMMARY

Army Form C. 2118.

| Place | Date | Hour | Summary of Events and Information | Remarks and references to Appendices |
|---|---|---|---|---|
| ACHIET | 19th July | | Considerable numbers of the enemy were killed and wounded by our machine guns firing S.N. not so much was done by the firing (S) to the rear as so difficult to fire little has been of the enemy in that direction. | |
| VILLERS | | | Within 15 minutes of the arrival of our men the enemy brought up two machine guns and deployed its opposite lp of the Coys formed for this move. It was then found that our own Artillery was firing to [illegible] about 2 to 3 of this enemy machine guns with the result that we're checked and when our advancing troops was within close range of the German the Royal Irish Regiment and S of our Machine Guns had succeeded the firing Over in turn was followed by the Middlesex Regiment but was from outset to been as Royal Dublin Fusiliers reached the position. In the left flank (A) our 2 oth the Lancs in Lancashire had the Greatest difficulties in the Sunken road and two Coys Reinforcement to the position. At 6.30 the 2 ordinance the line [illegible] | |

2449  Wt. W14957/M90  750,000  1/16  J.B.C. & A.  Forms/C.2118/12.

# WAR DIARY
## or
## INTELLIGENCE SUMMARY

Army Form C. 2118.

| Place | Date | Hour | Summary of Events and Information | Remarks and references to Appendices |
|---|---|---|---|---|
| AUCHON-VILLERS | 1st July 1916 | | Am at Mr Roston at my Pruno (O.O.) Stn. I Recd a message from Lieut. P.O. Byrne that I was to send to him to get forward with his guns owing to the congestion of the front line and tht Sergt Maclue Sub Sec tht was so playing on our flank. I therefore sent him a message to remain where he was & time ready to act on our Counter Attack. I also ordered 2nd Lieut Duffy to the Gun the Adjutant (Lieut McWilkinson) just along to the right of our line and re-organised out teams in the sector. On the retirement of our troops from the German lines I sent? rest for ammunition with the guns until the troops were back into our own line, then finding it impossible to remain intact and going no rate I out mune ammunition up to Mr Corbell to police around known the Group 16 men of the Genis he was reluctantly compelled destroy the Mischel already dug out out & return to a safer ground, enemy at 1300 the Coming Lancet finished informed me that he was going to re-inforce the Dublin Road with all the available men. At 1930 AT 1915. I opened media of fire on German fort lui trenches and continued until after the town was occupied the SUNKEN ROAD. | |

Army Form C. 2118.

# WAR DIARY
## or
## INTELLIGENCE SUMMARY
(Erase heading not required.)

| Place | Date | Hour | Summary of Events and Information | Remarks and references to Appendices |
|---|---|---|---|---|
| ACHIET-LES-VILLERS | 1st July | | Indices that our further attempt was to be made to go forward. I dropped my guns as follows:— | |
| | | | Oy toEnd 2 guns | |
| | | | Lawrence St 2 " | |
| | | | Bruay H " | |
| | | | OIR St 1 " | |
| | | | Essex St 1 " | |
| | | | New Trenches 1 " | |
| | | | Vicinity of Tr. 2 " | |
| | | | The column in position until the following day. During the night as much ammunition Bello Bros, share trails and inputs as possible was saved. Artillery fire from 12th sector was desultory. | |
| | 2nd July | | Artillery enemy 0805 fairly inactive throughout the day. Our Artillery was very active at 1500-1530 and 1830-1900. Also brought a lot of shell into fire from the enemy. During the day the 10th Brigade 4th Division relieved our 4th Artillery Guns | |

**Army Form C. 2118.**

# WAR DIARY
## or
## INTELLIGENCE SUMMARY
*(Erase heading not required.)*

Instructions regarding War Diaries and Intelligence Summaries are contained in F. S. Regs., Part II. and the Staff Manual respectively. Title Pages will be prepared in manuscript.

| Place | Date | Hour | Summary of Events and Information | Remarks and references to Appendices |
|---|---|---|---|---|
| AUCHON- VILLERS | 2nd July | | The Colonel Wancaghyn went to fire a gun could be placed in the vicinity of ST HELENS to command BEAUMONT ROAD approach the enemy getting through and his position no matter why hid. The Germans came in during the daylight with Red Cross flag and collected sent to be protective. | |
| | 3rd July | | Desultory fire was made by the Artillery on both sides. A reconnaissance aeroplane went into Enemy's lines by or the 4th Hants and my Rgt was given the S.O.S. Brigade HQ Div and the Rgt. Gave the S.O.S. Two teams were sent to occupy FOSS ROWS & WITHINGTON Trenches. Guns with teams returned to MAILLYWOOD. The Battery was in action during the period 1st—4th. LIEUT F.H. HART — 2/LIEUT J.O. LATER — 2/LIEUT G.M. CRESSEY all wounded. Capt LOVELL & 2/Lt AUGT REED Sergt LOVELL and 9 & 25 others wounded } not attacked. Missing 5. The following Officers N.C.O's mentioned good service throughout the engagement: Lieut F.J. McKILLOM, Lieut W.J. Wilcox 1230045 Bombardier. O.C. Lovell. 20917 Sergt P. Banks. 2011 Dr. Armstrong and 9349 Dr. J.C. Chandler. The whole Brigade worked exceeding well during a very trying time. | |

Army Form C. 2118.

# WAR DIARY
## or
## INTELLIGENCE SUMMARY
*(Erase heading not required.)*

| Place | Date | Hour | Summary of Events and Information | Remarks and references to Appendices |
|---|---|---|---|---|
| MAILLY | 5th July 1916 | | A further two machine guns were sent into the front line. All guns, ammunition and spare parts obtained their quota from Ordnance. | |
| MAILLY | 6th-7th | | During operations was released from Ordnance. Machine gun included. No further attempts were made on our front to push again Company Engaged in cleaning & overhauling prisoners to taking over new front line from MARY REDAN & R ANCRE the more to take place night of 8th-9th. The Brigade Lewis Gun Company (Captain E. Sackett) has been posted to the 8th I. Brigade in Staff Captain Lieut D.N. McRuvie assumed command and Lieut. S.G. 2nd Lieut purr took over duties of 2nd in command. 2 Lieut. Thurion M.G. Corps was posted to the Bde army from the Base 7th inst. | |

Owen Bethune McLean
Lieut Cd"d O the Bde M G Company
7th July 1916

Army Form C. 2118.

# WAR DIARY
## or
## INTELLIGENCE SUMMARY

(Erase heading not required.)

| Place | Date | Hour | Summary of Events and Information | Remarks and references to Appendices |
|---|---|---|---|---|
| ACHEUX | 7.7.16 | | Captain Birdwood this day appointed Staff Captain to the 86th Brigade, and under instructions from the Brigade, Lieut. H.V. Wilkinson took over command of the 86th Brigade Machine Gun Coy. | |
| " | 8.7.16 | | In the ENGLEBELMER sector the enemy's artillery has been less active. Some shrapnel & small H.E. were fired during the night into our right sub sector and ENGLEBURMER was slightly shelled during the morning. Our own artillery was very active during the night on the German Trenches. In the AUCHONVILLERS sector occasional rounds of 150 M.M. were fired on AUCHONVILLERS & SUCRERIE about midnight. 4 bombs from a heavy trench mortar fell near JACOB'S LADDER without doing any damage. In the ENGLE BELMER sector the enemy fired on our aeroplanes with M.G.s from well behind their front line. Three patrols went out from our lines during the night; no hostile patrols were encountered. | |

# WAR DIARY
## or
## INTELLIGENCE SUMMARY

Army Form C. 2118.

| Place | Date | Hour | Summary of Events and Information | Remarks and references to Appendices |
|---|---|---|---|---|
| | 8.7.16 (contd) | | This Brigade relieved the 87th Brigade in the firing line, taking over from MARY REDAN on the north, to the RIVER ANCRE on the south. Lt McALPIN & 2/Lt FURNISS with 5 guns in the vicinity of SHOOTERS HILL, and 2/Lt DUFFY with 3 guns to JACOBS LADDER. Weather cloudy with bright intervals. | |
| | 9.7.16 | | At 1902 a B.E. 2.3 was brought down by a FOKKER over MIRAUMONT. The fokker appeared to dive almost vertically at the B.E.2.3 which was seen to crash to the ground about L 34. D. 4. I. Another of our aeroplanes was attacked about the same time over ACHIET-LE-GRAND. Numbers of Germans throughout the day were seen walking in the open, apparently to avoid water logged trenches. The enemy was hard at work most of the day repairing trenches. On being shelled they stopped work, but continued again at intervals | |

# WAR DIARY
## or
## INTELLIGENCE SUMMARY

Army Form C. 2118.

| Place | Date | Hour | Summary of Events and Information | Remarks and references to Appendices |
|---|---|---|---|---|
| | 9.7.16 | (contd) | Went all round the line with the General & chose a new M.G position. 2nd Lt J St Eapon this day joined from Base, and is taken on the strength of this unit. Moved Hd Quarters from MAILLY to dug-outs in KNIGHTS BRIDGE. Two guns from the yellow line returned to H.Q. MAILLY leaving two guns up only. Weather sunny. Humid, but cold at night. | |
| | 10.7.16 | | Enemy artillery was registering on NEW TRENCH, and also put some heavy shrapnel in our front line. MESNIL & HAMEL were shelled intermittently during the day & night. Our artillery active throughout the day & especially at night between 2300 + 0200. One of our Balloons near ALBERT was seen to | |

# WAR DIARY
## or
## INTELLIGENCE SUMMARY

Army Form C.2118.

| Place | Date | Hour | Summary of Events and Information | Remarks and references to Appendices |
|---|---|---|---|---|
| | 10.7.16 | (Cont) | came down in flames at 18.45. Volumes of black smoke that looked like a fire seen in the direction of POZIERES. There appeared to be a fire also in ALBERT in the afternoon. | |
| | | | One R.E. corporal + 3 sappers attached to this unit for assisting to build new M.G. emplacements. | |
| | | | Lieut Byrne returned to MAILLY. 2Lt Orpen + two dismd to about G.23.B.90.50 to build 2 new gun pits. Lieut Milne relieved Lieut McAlpin at SHOOTERS HILL and the latter returned to Hd Qrs at KNIGHTSBRIDGE as 2nd in command & adjutant. | |
| | | | Weather. Bright sunshine, clear air. | |
| | 11.7.16 | | Except in the HEBUTERNE Sector where there was a slight demonstration | |

Army Form C. 2118.

# WAR DIARY
## or
## INTELLIGENCE SUMMARY
(Erase heading not required.)

| Place | Date | Hour | Summary of Events and Information | Remarks and references to Appendices |
|---|---|---|---|---|
| | 11.7.16 (contd) | | of artillery, the hostile artillery maintained an intermittent and in places fairly heavy fire through the day & night. a number of tear shells & on K 34 B & D were smoke shells. In the ENGLEBURMER sector the enemy shelled our front line with heavy shrapnel, causing some damage, especially round CONSTITUTION HILL. A German M G played continuously on sap leading from trench 9 & 7. during the night. During June the German losses of aeroplanes, captured & destroyed are 46 machines. Weather, sunny, somewhat windy. Met the C.O. of the 147th Brigade machine Gun Coy. (on next section on our right) and took him round our positions, showing him the 6 guns covering his front. | |

Army Form C. 2118.

# WAR DIARY
## or
## INTELLIGENCE SUMMARY
(Erase heading not required.)

| Place | Date | Hour | Summary of Events and Information | Remarks and references to Appendices |
|---|---|---|---|---|
| | 12.7.16 | | Enemy artillery active, chiefly H.E. on front line, & shrapnel over HAMEL. MESNIL was also shelled during the day, & at odd intervals during the night. A hostile aeroplane was driven off by two of ours during afternoon. Around our trenches all morning looking for new positions. The C.O. of the 13th motor Machine Gun Battery came up at 15.00, showed him part of the line & chose two positions for him to mount two guns for offensive work only - indirect fire - Weather, overcast & raw. | |
| | 13.7.16 | 4h at 4 a.m. and met the C.O. 147th Brigade, and went over part of his line at THIEPVAL, chose two positions where he could bring fire to bear on the German front line trenches on our right front, as we are not able to do so satisfactory from our sector. Recced our own lines & positions all morning | |

# WAR DIARY or INTELLIGENCE SUMMARY

Army Form C. 2118.

| Place | Date | Hour | Summary of Events and Information | Remarks and references to Appendices |
|---|---|---|---|---|
| | 13.7.16 (Contd) | | No 1 Section 13" mortar Machine Gun Battery (2 guns) arrived at 2200 and immediately started on their emplacements. Enemy artillery very active from 2230 to 2345. H.E. shrapnel + Trench mortars on front line + NEW TRENCH. Our aeroplanes flying very low over Enemy's lines, but Enemy batteries do not appear to open machine gun fire on them, being content with a small amount of rifle fire. At 2200 on discharge of our gas, we opened heavy M.G. fire on Boschés front + communication trenches. | |
| | 14.7.16 | | A draft of 1 corporal + 14 gunners this day arrived. We opened up a heavy artillery + machine gun bombardment at 0315 to 0345 on all trenches & at 0330 smoke was discharged in order to keep the Germans on the alert, whilst the IV Army attacked further SOUTH. From today onwards 3 times in every 24 hours there is to be a 10 minutes bombardment on the German trenches by artillery + machine guns. Went normal all guns + persistent during the day. | |

Army Form C. 2118.

# WAR DIARY
## or
## INTELLIGENCE SUMMARY
(Erase heading not required.)

Instructions regarding War Diaries and Intelligence Summaries are contained in F.S. Regs., Part II. and the Staff Manual respectively. Title Pages will be prepared in manuscript.

| Place | Date | Hour | Summary of Events and Information | Remarks and references to Appendices |
|---|---|---|---|---|
| | 16-7-16 | | Our artillery fairly active throughout day & night. Our machine guns playing on German Communication trenches at intervals through day & night. Lt Byrne relieved 2/Lt Duffy at JACOBS LADDER. 5 Teams in vicinity of SHOOTERS HILL & 2 teams in YELLOW LINE were relieved by seven teams from MAILLY MAILLY. Dull cold morning. Rain afternoon & throughout night. | |
| | 17-7-16 | | ALBERT HALL & KNIGHTSBRIDGE leaving shelled from 2300 to 0100 (17-7-16) with gas shells. Germans evidently going for the Batteries but these did 2/3 came in to the full benefit. An 2000 shells falling in a very small radius. The gas did not give perfect satisfaction. A new M.G. emplacement in SHOOTERS HILL which was practically completed received a direct hit from a "crump" smashing the sand rails of the roof in pieces - position abandoned. - A Draft of 3 L/Cpls & 11 Gunners arrived from England. The Worcester Regt raided the Boches Trenches, but | |

2449 Wt. W14957/M90 750,000 1/16 J.B.C. & A. Forms/C.2118/12.

**Army Form C. 2118.**

# WAR DIARY
## or
## INTELLIGENCE SUMMARY

*(Erase heading not required.)*

Instructions regarding War Diaries and Intelligence Summaries are contained in F. S. Regs., Part II. and the Staff Manual respectively. Title Pages will be prepared in manuscript.

| Place | Date | Hour | Summary of Events and Information | Remarks and references to Appendices |
|---|---|---|---|---|
| | 17/7/16 | (cont) | only two officers & a corporal got in and after shooting 2 Germans & bombing a dug-out had to retire. | |
| | 18/7/16 | | 4th Batt. relieved at SHOOTERS HILL by 2nd Lt Duffy. When the R.E's were out in front wiring, they discovered a flare running from the enemies wire to our own. They pulled this in and used it themselves. A small enemy patrol was seen and dispersed by Lewis gun fire. It looked as if a raid was going to take place that night. Weather bright & sunny. | |
| | 21/7/16 | | At 2330 there was a heavy Bombardment, considerable damage being done. It lasted until 0130. Weather bright & fine. Finished two new gun emplacements. | |
| | 22/7/16 | | | |
| | 24/7/16 | | The Company were relieved by the 7th Bn M G Coy at 1400 all completed by 16.30 and marched back to MAILLY by sections. Left MAILLY at 18.45 and marched to BUS arriving there 20.15 and remained there for the night in the wood. Weather fine. | |

# WAR DIARY
## or
## INTELLIGENCE SUMMARY

*(Erase heading not required.)*

Army Form C. 2118.

| Place | Date | Hour | Summary of Events and Information | Remarks and references to Appendices |
|---|---|---|---|---|
| | 25.7.16 | | The whole Company left BUS at 0900 and marched to BEAUVAL arriving there at 15.30. Weather bright sunshine. Lieut H.V. WILKINSON promoted Captain on taking over Command of the Company to take from 2nd inst. Lieut T.A BYRNE promoted Captain (Special reserve) dated 7th March 1916. | |
| | 26.7.16 | | The whole Company cleaning guns, arms, & ammunition, and mr packing limbers. Weather fine. | |
| | 27.7.16 | | The Company marched from BEAUVAL to WORMHOUDT, one section & its transport with each Battalion. No 2 Section left BEAUVAL 0800 entrained at DOULLONS 11.34. detrained at ESQUELBECK at 17.10 and marched to billets, 2.7 kilometres fast WORMHOUDT arriving there at 19..10. followed by nos 1 3 & 4 sections, last section arriving at 0630 (28.7.16) Weather fine. | |
| | 29.7.16 | | Physical drill before breakfast Parades 0900 to 12.30 cleaning guns etc & packing limbers afternoon. Showery weather. | |

Army Form C.2118.

# WAR DIARY
## or
## INTELLIGENCE SUMMARY

(Erase heading not required.)

Instructions regarding War Diaries and Intelligence Summaries are contained in F. S. Regs., Part II. and the Staff Manual respectively. Title Pages will be prepared in manuscript.

| Place | Date | Hour | Summary of Events and Information | Remarks and references to Appendices |
|---|---|---|---|---|
| | 30.7.16 | | Left NORMHOUDT L.45. Marched to POPERINGE about 4 miles and took over the huts vacated by the 18th Brigade Machine Gun Coy. Transport by road arrived 15.50. Weather very hot. | |
| | 31.7.16 | | This Company in reserve. Parades, cleaning & clearing up, all occupied all day. Weather beautiful | |

M.W.Wilkinson
Capt.
Comdg 86th Machine Gun Coy.

31st July 1916.

## 86th Machine Gun Company

### Casualty Roll to date

| Batts N°. | Rank & Name | Nature of Casualty | Remarks |
|---|---|---|---|
|  | Lieut. Hardy, F.N. | Wounded |  |
|  | 2/Lieut. Later J.O. | do | Died of wounds July 13th |
|  | do. Creasy G.M. | do |  |
| 20970 | Sergt Dunn W. | Killed |  |
| 20920 | Corpl Lovell A.M. | do |  |
| 20909 | Pte Barlow H. | do |  |
| 20948 | " Crannie B. | do |  |
| 20978 | " Jennie J. | do |  |
| 20955 | " McIntyre R. | do |  |
| 20918 | Sergt Lovell A.D. | Wounded |  |
| 21002 | " White J. | " |  |
| 20973 | Corpl McNab W. | " |  |
| 21019 | L/Cpl Byrne W. | " |  |
| 20949 | Pte Burke P. | " |  |
| 20923 | " Cox J. | " |  |
| 20955 | " Duggan J. | " |  |
| 20931 | " Davies W. | " |  |
| 20928 | " Francis P. | " |  |
| 21031 | " Freeman J. | " |  |
| 20987 | " Henrich L. | " |  |
| 1973 | " Howe B. | " |  |
| 20918 | " Bardon J. | " |  |

Continued

## Casualty Roll, continued

| Book No. | Rank & Name | Nature of Casualty | Remarks |
|---|---|---|---|
| 20989 | Pte Lewis L. | Wounded | |
| 20998 | " Lynch F. | " | |
| 21001 | " O'Brien J. | " | |
| 20956 | " O'Callaghan J. | " | |
| 20933 | " Parkins E. | " | |
| 21034 | " Parsons H. | " | |
| 20969 | " Perrin C. | " | |
| 20903 | " Singleton J. | " | |
| 20966 | " Tinsley A. | " | |
| 20926 | Pte Finn H. | Missing | |
| 11643 | " Fulton W. | " | |

### Attached

| Book No. | Rank & Name | Nature of Casualty | Remarks |
|---|---|---|---|
| 15467 | Pte Bugg V. | Wounded | 2nd Royal Fus. |
| 1327 | " Deaton B. | " | " |
| 9296 | " Halagoda A. | " | " |
| 3720 | " O'Brien J. | " | 1st Lancs. Fus. |
| 4508 | " Redfern A. | " | " |
| 26457 | " Simpson H. | " | " |
| 1859 | " Jones A.P. | " | 16th Middlesex |

## No 1 Section

① Lieut. W. F. McAlpin

| | | | |
|---|---|---|---|
| 20917 | Sgt | Shanks | P. |
| 20934 | Pte | George | S. |
| 20927 | " | Low | W. |
| 20930 | " | Pemberton | D. |
| 20926 | " | Finn | H. |
| 20955 | " | Duggan | J. |
| 3619 | " | Hockett | F. |
| 21034 | " | Parsons | H. |
| | (Off scout) | | |

② 

| | | | |
|---|---|---|---|
| 20920 | Corpl | Lovell | A.W. |
| 20923 | Pte | Cox | G. |
| 20907 | " | Hulett | E. |
| 20933 | " | Watkins | D. |
| 20932 | " | Purcell | A. |
| 1327 | " | Denton | T. |
| 15467 | " | Kingg | V. |

③ Lieut. F.H. Hardy

| | | | |
|---|---|---|---|
| 20918 | Sergt | Lovell | A.B. |
| 20921 | L/C. | Titmarsh | W. |
| 20904 | Pte | Waldron | W. |
| 20936 | " | Pyatt | W. |
| 20903 | " | Singleton | J. |
| 11643 | " | Fulton | N. |
| 5011 | " | Ainsworth | L. |
| 20908 | " | Pretty | H. |
| | (Off scout) | | |

④

| | | | |
|---|---|---|---|
| 20919 | L/Sgt | Bussard | N. |
| 20907 | Pte | Barlow | H. |
| 20931 | " | Davies | W. |
| 20905 | " | Finnell | W. |
| 20929 | " | Revell | P. |
| 9349 | " | Chandler | J. |
| 12800 | " | Woolridge | A. |

## No. 2 Section

Lieut. J. Stevenson     2/Lt. J.O. Later

| | | | | | |
|---|---|---|---|---|---|
| 20971 | Sergt Duffy | J. | 20770 | Sergt Bunn | W |
| 20977 | Pte Wood | J. | 20982 | Pte Edwards | J.P. |
| 20950 | " Hannafin | T | 20949 | " Burke | P |
| 20988 | " Cave | A | 20975 | " Morgan | C. |
| 20966 | " Tinsley | A | 20944 | " Kelly | J.T |
| 15924 | " Conlon | J | 3248 | " Bailey | |
| 3778 | " O'Connor | T | 3720 | " O'Brien | Jos. |
| 20997 | " Hogan (Off. Servant) | W | 20998 | " Lynch (Off. Servant) | J. |

| | | | | | |
|---|---|---|---|---|---|
| 20945 | Corpl O'Connell | P | 20973 | Cpl McNab | W |
| 20979 | Pte Shaw | H. | 20990 | Pte Allan | S |
| 20987 | " Derrick | L | 20978 | " Lennie | T |
| 2968 | " Hanbury | J. | 20969 | " Devin | C. |
| 4508 | " Redfern | A. | 20987 | " Lewis | L. |
| 5198 | " Holt | M | 20983 | " Colman | M |
| 12296 | " Charlesworth | J | 10503 | " Candlish | J |
| 20964 | " Stanway (Signaller) | F. | | | |

## No. III Section

**⑨ 2/Lt G.H. Greasey**

| | | |
|---|---|---|
| 21002 | Sergt White | J |
| 20956 | Pte O'Callaghan | J |
| 20951 | " Murphy | W |
| 20955 | " McIntyre | R |
| 7872 | " Wood | D |
| 8336 | " Hoyle | J |
| 2354 | " Farncombe | D |
| 20959 | " O'Brien P. (Off Servant) | |

**⑪ 2/Lt D.J. Duffy**

| | | |
|---|---|---|
| 20922 | Corpl Fletcher | B |
| 20947 | Clarke | L |
| 20953 | Regan | W |
| 20951 | Hunt | A |
| 20946 | Murphy | E |
| 5874 | Osborne | T |
| 1859 | Jones | A |
| 20963 | Foster (Off Servant) | R |

**⑩**

| | | |
|---|---|---|
| 20942 | Sergt Sparling | W |
| 20948 | Pte Brannie | B |
| 20952 | " Noonan | W |
| 11714 | " Whitwall | C |
| 1973 | " Howe | B |
| 2368 | " Longnie | A |
| 2460 | " Stevens | H |

**⑫**

| | | |
|---|---|---|
| 20943 | Corpl Murphy | A |
| 20954 | Pte McSweeney | T |
| 20958 | " O'Brien | M |
| 14009 | " Tiffin | A |
| 9403 | " O'Reilly | R |
| 1424 | " Stone | J |
| 1423 | " Stone | H |
| 20965 | " Wild (Squaller) | R |

## No. IV Section

Lieut W. Moilue                    Lieut P. A. Byrne

**(13)**                           **(15)**

| | | | |
|---|---|---|---|
| 20972 Sergt McDougall J. | | 21003 Sergt Ronan W |
| 21013 Pte Hughes M | | 21017 Pte Fish N |
| 21014 " King J. | | 21015 " McAuley M |
| 21007 " Doyle J | | 21030 " Merlin T |
| 21025 " Gane W | | 21009 " Fanning B. |
| 9088 " Windle A | | 9087 " Wilson F |
| 22012 " Elliott J. | | 9597 " McGuckin J |
| 21032 " Purcell J | | 21031 " Freeman J |
| (Off Servant) | | (Off Servant) |

**(14)**                           **(16)**

| | | | |
|---|---|---|---|
| 21004 Corpl Doyle P | | 21005 Corpl Norris R. |
| 21016 Pte McDermott R | | 21010 Pte Gorey J |
| 21012 " Kenny J | | 21011 " Jones D |
| 21020 " Black J. | | 20918 " Borda J |
| 21008 " Dean J. | | 21019 4/8 Byrne J |
| 18597 " Reilly D. | | 8847 Pte O'Toole J |
| 21023 " Byrne L | | 9385 " Butter J |
| 20901 " Bowes F | | |
| (Signaller) | | |

## Head Quarters

|       | Captain Beckwith | O.C. |
|-------|------------------|------|
|       | Lieut. Wilkinson | Adj  |
| 21033 | Pte Gibbs S.     | Orderly |
| 21000 | " Redmont T      | - " - |
| 20916 | " Daily J        | Servant |
| 21036 | " Walker T       | - " - |

### Brigade H.Qrs.

| 11315 | Corpl Bolton A. | Signaller |

### Under I.S.M.

| 20898 | I.S.M. Digby W |
| 4518 | Sergt Fenner A |
| 9056 | - " - Nolan J |
| 15122 | Corpl White H. |
| 4518 | - " - Collins D |
| 20914 | L/Cpl Byard S. |
| 15535 | Pte Westgarth H. |
| 9296 | " Halangado A. |
| 2763 | " Richardson H. |
| 26457 | " Simpson H |
| 21815 | " Kearns P. |
| 3894 | " Dwyer M. |
| 9116 | " Leggitt W |

### Under C.O.M.S.

| 20899 | Q.M.S. Sullivan T |
| 20925 | L/Cpl Moovid J. |
| 20984 | Pte Knowles J |
| 20915 | " Howell J |
| 21001 | " O'Brien J |
| 20902 | " Pullen J. |

# SECRET

REFERENCE
- △ GRENADES
- □ S.A.A.
- △ T.M. Ammunition
- ○ RATIONS
- ⌑ Water in Tins
- " Supply & TANKS
- ○ R.E Stores
- ▨ Regt Aid posts
- ▣ ADV. Dressing Stn.
- ⊟ Signal Stn.
- ▨ Brigade HQ

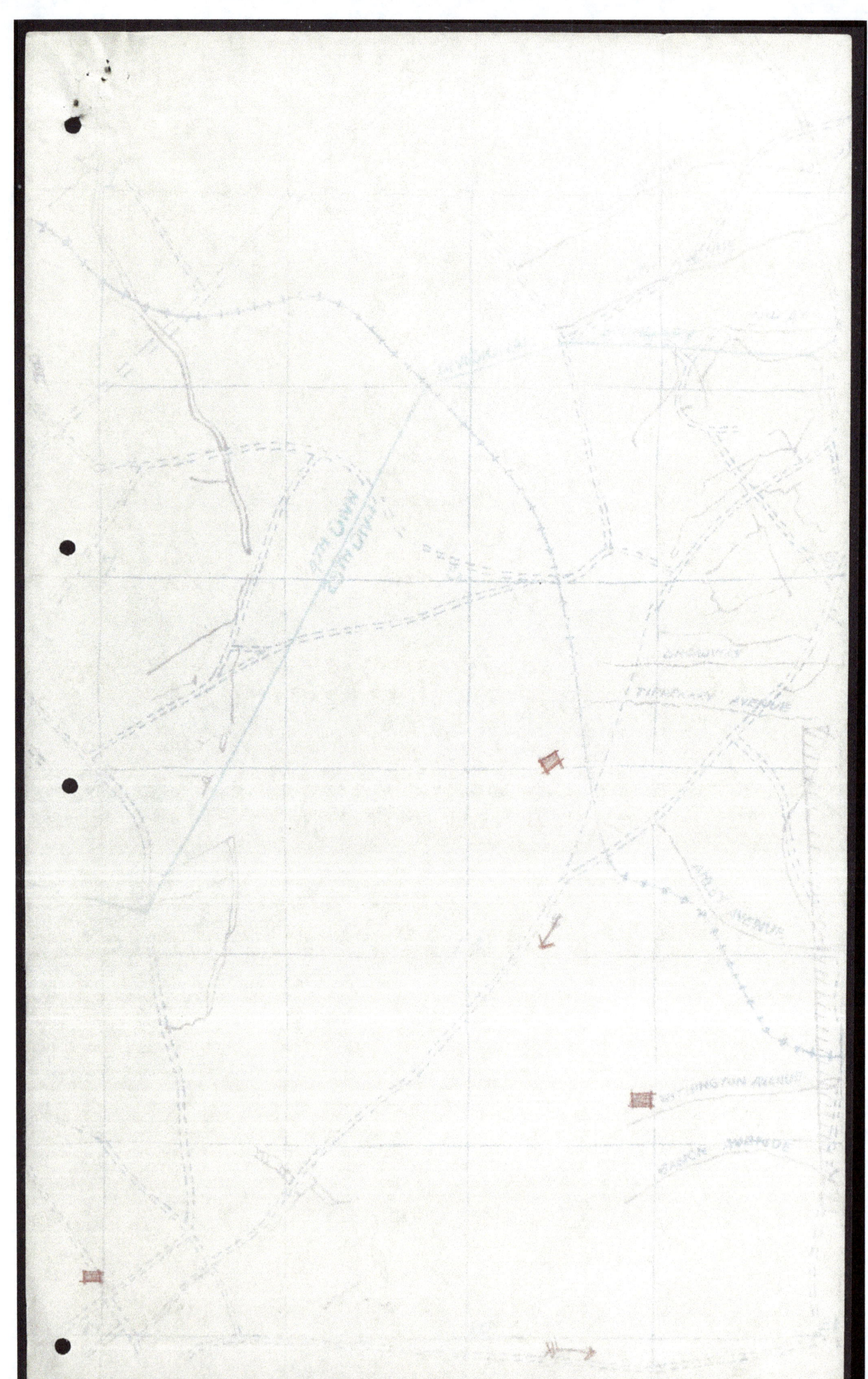

Secret                                                                Copy No. 16.

## 86th Bde Machine Gun Co.
## Operation Order.

Reference 1/20,000 57.D.S.E.
         1/10,000 Trench map Sheet 57.D.S.E.
         Beaumont (1 and 2 parts).

The 29th Division is to take part in an attack on the enemy's trenches, on a date to be notified later, which will be indicated in these orders by the letter "Z".

**1. Objective of 86th Brigade.**

The area allotted to the 86th Brigade is:-
Northern Boundary:- Q.5.c.2.8. to Q.6.c.5.4.
Southern    "    :- Q.10.d.6.8. to Q.12.b.7.5.

**2. Allocation of guns U.V.W.X & Y days**

| Positions | No. | Commander |
|---|---|---|
| Bowery | 2 | Lt. J.F.B. Stevenson |
| Pilk Street | 1 | " W. Milne |
| Essex Street | 1 | |
| Newtownards | 1 | " D.J.E. DUFFY. |
| "P" Street | 1 | |

**3. "Z" day**

At -10 Stokes Mortars open hurricane bombardment and vicinity of ⊙ becomes crater. Immediately following this, No.1 Section (4 guns) under Lieuts F.K. McAlpin and F.H. Hardy push over the HAWTHORNE REDOUBT there establish their guns. 2 guns engage German trenches running N. & 2 guns engage those going "S". These guns should be in position at 0.0.

When the 4 Royal Fus. pass through them they will immediately come under the orders of the O.C. that unit.

Should these guns become neutralised, the Gun Commander will report to the O.C. Brigade Machine Gun Co. who will give instructions for their further employment.

"Z" day
(continued)

2 Guns of No. 2 Section under 2/Lieut. J.O. LATER will be attached to 2/Lancashire Fusiliers and under the orders of the Offr. Comdg that Unit.

2 Guns of No. 3 Section under Lieut. G.M. CREASEY will advance at 0.0 on the left of the LANCS FUSRS push round them and establish themselves at (62) getting a Vertical searching fire on (23) - (24) with one gun and on (66) with the other and continue fire till 1.20 observer must be put out to watch advancing troops and fire effect. At 1.25 move guns forward to (33) establish and range on (15) and S.E. Q.6.a.9.a and wire beyond.

2 Guns under Lieut P.A. BYRNE will advance on the Right of the 2/Royal Fusrs reaching a point Q.11.a.4.8 one gun engaging BEAUMONT ALLEY and one (11) to (98) these guns will be re-inforced at 0.20 by 2 Guns under Lieut. D.J.P. DUFFY.

At 1.00 traversing fire will be kept up between (111) - (5) lifting fire at 1.15.

At 1.25 all 4 guns move forward as rapidly as possible to (98) establishing and covering our troops who will be wire cutting from R.7.A.6.2. to R.1.c.26.56.

At 0.20 the guns from the BOWERY, ESSEX ST, and PILK ST. with O.C. Company will advance across the German trenches through & Cemetery Q.11.d.2.7. to Right of 2nd Objective.

4.
FIRE

DIV: OPER. ORDER 36 para 11 and 24.
Bde OPER. ORDER 55 para 24.
 "     "      "    appendix "7" No. d. (Gas)
 "     "      "    No. 56 para 3 Reconnaissance

5.
SAFETY

Guns will cease overhead fire as soon as our assaulting troops are near our Unit of Safety

**Safety (continued)** — 2 degrees of safety (Tangent sights raised 400 yards) will be used.

All guns must be prepared to cover our flanks in case of counter attack.

**6. Rate of Fire** — During hours that guns are firing, every gun will fire at least 1 belt every 20 minutes.

**7. Headquarters** — 86th Brigade junction of Essex St & Broadway
Machine Gun " . Pilk St & Cardiff trench

**8. Communication.** — Telephone between:-
Machine Gun Hqrs.
Brigade Head qrs.
Bowery
Newtownards.

Runners will be with M.G. Headquarters. All officers servants will act as runners to their officers.

After M.G. Headqrs have moved forward, signallers will collect up instruments and move forward and establish communication from the German 2nd line.

**9. Ammunition Supply S.A.A.** — Each gun N° going forward will carry a short length belt (25 rounds) in his belt or any handy position.

```
7. team. short belts ............ 175
N.C.O. one box .................. 250
No 1 and 2 . each ............... 500
No 3, 4 & 6 two box each ........ 1500
    Total going over with gun - 2425
```

Ammunition dumps are established at:-
King St., Pilk St, 1st Avenue

The company reserve of 4500 rounds per gun

**A.A.** (2.000) will be divided on 4 limbers ready to move forward when required.

Officers in charge of teams will personally assure themselves that their ammunition carriers are thoroughly acquainted with these Dumps and also their duties.

There are also spare belts packed 2 in a sandbag at these Dumps, the bags are marked with a black circle ⭕ on both sides of bags.

**PISTOL** Pistol ammunition can be obtained from the C.S.M.

**BOMBS.** 2 bombs per man will be carried by those Nos. who do not carry rifles.

**WATER** A plentiful supply of water must be maintained at each gun till "Z" day. Then Commanders of guns must see their carriers bring up water.

Teams must be cautioned about drinking water from wells etc. in the former lines, till it has been tested to see if it is fit for drinking and cooking.

**RATIONS** Rations will be issued as usual until "Z" day. On "Z" day rations for the Company will be drawn direct from re-filling point in the cooks carts and will move forward under instructions received from Brigade.

If circumstances permit, the ration train will proceed to MAILLY WOOD on "Z" day. The re-filling point for the following day will be on the MAILLY - HEDAUVILLE road alongside MAILLY WOOD close to troughs or will act if the wire.

**DISTINGUISHING MARKS** All ranks except numbers ready to

**15. GAS** (continued).
 to see that their Gas Sprayers are in good working order, and that additional jars of Solution are available. The Company Gas N.C.O. has been sent round these Sprayers, but Officers are responsible they are ready for use.

Great care must be taken of the Box respirators, and attention is called to Circular re "Alternative Method of Wearing Anti-Gas helmets during Gas Alert."

**16. Kits, Stores and Orderly Room documents.**
All officers will carry with them what they require, Gun numbers are not to carry anything but their own Kit and the material required for the work allotted to them.

All Officers Kits will be securely rolled up in their Kit bags or Valises plainly marked with owners name etc, inside and out.

These will be stored at the Company Dump at ACHEUX.

All Company stores will be packed in boxes or packs and placed in Company Dump under charge of C.Q.M.S. and S/Sgt Morris.

Mens Overcoats rolled in bundles of 5 together with their packs will be stored in the cellar No 3 Billet in MAILLY MAILLET.

**17. MEDICAL**
All troops are reminded that the care of the wounded is the duty of Regimental Stretcher bearers and Field Ambulances, fighting troops are forbidden to accompany wounded men to the Dressing Stations.

**18. LOOTING**
Looting is a Court Martial Crime punishable by Death.

**GUNS IN
DANGER OF CAPTURE.**    Gun Commanders will instruct their men
how to render a Machine Gun useless, in the
event of a gun being in danger of being
captured.

20
**IMPORTANCE OF
THE ATTACK**     It is of the utmost importance for
this attack to be successful and all Officers
N.C.O's and men must exert their maximum
effort to make the attack a success and upon
the energy and cheerfulness of the Officers largely
depends the success of the engagement.

**TROOPS HOLDING
FRONT LINE**     During the bombardment the Brigade
front will be held by 2 Companies of Royal
Fusiliers and 2 companies Lancashire Fusiliers.

22
**ROUTE**     On Y/Z night the Company will move
from ACHEUX by the following route:-
    ROTTEN ROW    } Point P.8.d.80.45. where ROTTEN
    NEW TRACK     } ROW leaves ACHEUX WOOD by 21.40
    BROADWAY      } above mentioned point to be
    2nd AVENUE    } cleared by 21.45

23
**PROGRAMME OF
INFANTRY ADVANCE**    See Brigade Operation Order Appendix 3
(issued separately)

24
**PRISONERS**    Any Prisoners taken will be escorted
back to our original front line and handed
over to O.C. _____ to be informed.

25
**TRANSPORT**    The Transport Officer will draw the
Company the _____ Cookers and _____
Pack Ponies from _____ on taking orders from
                                    the Brigade

Trench           On "Z" day communication trenches
traffic          will be reserved as follows:-
                 UP traffic  Withington, Tipperary and 6d Avenue.
                 DOWN   "    Gabion Avenue, Broadway

                                    Edgell/with.      Captain,
                                    Commanding 86th Bde
                                                Machine Gun Coy.

Copy No 1 & 2   Office
        3.      War Diary
        4.      86th Brigade
        5.  Lt  McAlpin K.F.
        6.   "  Hardy A.F.
        7.   "  Stevenson J.B.F.
        8.  2/Lt Later J.O.
        9.   "  Creasey G.M.
       10.   "  Duffy D.J.P.
       11. Lt  Milne W.
       12.  "  Byrne P.A.
       13. C.S.M. Digby W.

In the Field.
June 23rd 1916.

29th Division.
86th Infantry Brigade
------

86th BRIGADE

MACHINE GUN COMPANY

AUGUST 1 9 1 6

Vol 7

Confidential
War Diary
— of —
86th Co. Machine Gun Corps.

From 1st August to 31st August
— 1916 —

— Volume 7. —

Army Form C. 2118.

# 80th Machine Gun Company.

# WAR DIARY
## or
## INTELLIGENCE SUMMARY
(Erase heading not required.)

Instructions regarding War Diaries and Intelligence Summaries are contained in F. S. Regs., Part II. and the Staff Manual respectively. Title Pages will be prepared in manuscript.

| Place | Date | Hour | Summary of Events and Information | Remarks and references to Appendices |
|---|---|---|---|---|
| BRANDHOEK | 1.8.16 | | A draft of N.C.O.s were posted to, and taken on the strength of this Company on the 31st July 1916. | |
| | | | Reveille at 5 a.m. Brigade route march 7 a.m. other Parades. | |
| | | 09.15 to 10.00 | Rifle Drill | |
| | | 10.15 to 12.30 | New drafts for gun instruction, remainder of Company, under Section Officers, drill etc. | |
| | | | Gas helmet drill & examination. | |
| | | 14.00 | One section on the range. | |
| | | 17.00 | | |
| | | | Weather fine & warm | |
| | 6.8.16 | | Brigade sports at 15.00. Concert by this Company 19.00. | |
| | 7.8.16 | | The weather has remained fine & warm all the time we were in reserve. The health of the Company was fair, about 8% of the Coy being admitted to Hospital, owing chiefly to the strain |

Army Form C. 2118. 2

# WAR DIARY
## or
## INTELLIGENCE SUMMARY
*(Erase heading not required.)*

Instructions regarding War Diaries and Intelligence Summaries are contained in F. S. Regs., Part II. and the Staff Manual respectively. Title Pages will be prepared in manuscript.

| Place | Date | Hour | Summary of Events and Information | Remarks and references to Appendices |
|---|---|---|---|---|
| | 7.8.16 | (Contd) | of the previous 5 weeks. They stuck it out whilst in the trenches, but the reaction afterwards to be taken nowhere. Company considerably smartened up. all Officers & Section Sergeants have been over the new lines in front of YPRES. Every man, including cooks, signallers etc, have fired on the ranges. | |
| YPRES | 8.8.16 | | This Company relieved the 78th M.G. Coy in the line at YPRES. relief not completed until 4.30 a.m. owing chiefly to the Germans discharging much gas. all horses & mules were heavily shelled as well as YPRES. no casualties:- Transport 1 man killed, L/Cpl severely wounded, 1 man wounded, one horse killed & mules wounded. In the trams two men gassed. The Battalion on the right sector had about 200 casualties. Bosche attempted an attack on our left. | |

Army Form C.2118.

# WAR DIARY
## or
## INTELLIGENCE SUMMARY

(Erase heading not required.)

| Place | Date | Hour | Summary of Events and Information | Remarks and references to Appendices |
|---|---|---|---|---|
| YPRES | 8.8.16 | | which was stopped but no attack or raid on our front. Guns as follows:- <br> No 1 Section, 2/Lt Cohen in reserve at Hd Qts Canal Banks <br> " 2 " D/Lt Furniss, vicinity of Wieltje <br> " 3 " 2/Lt Duffy — Potijze <br> " 4 " Capt Byrne — St Jean | |
| | 9.8.16 | | Round the whole of our gun positions & adjutant (Lt McAffer) all day. Weather fine & very hot. 2nd Lieut Furniss evacuated, suffering from gas poisoning, also 1 man. The ill effects did not come on until 17 hours afterwards. | |
| | 10.8.16 | | 2nd Lieut Cohen took charge of the guns in the line in place of 2/Lt Furniss. Beautiful weather & a quiet day. | |

Army Form C. 2118.

# WAR DIARY
## or
## INTELLIGENCE SUMMARY

(Erase heading not required.)

| Place | Date | Hour | Summary of Events and Information | Remarks and references to Appendices |
|---|---|---|---|---|
| YPRES | 28th | | Capt Osgone admitted to Hospital with fever Influenza Bombardment on our right from 09.00 to 10.15. Instructed to take over the 43" Machine Gun Company. Handed over all documents & the Company to Capt E. Beckwith on his reporting. | |

A.W.Wilkinson
Capt.
Cmdg 86th M.G.C.

# WAR DIARY or INTELLIGENCE SUMMARY

| Place | Date | Hour | Summary of Events and Information | Remarks and references to Appendices |
|---|---|---|---|---|
| YPRES | 1916 12 Aug | | Captain Beckwith accompanied C.S.O.2 round line with a view to selecting positions for Strong Points and Gun Emplacements. Night was quiet, our Machine Guns fired on enemy communication trenches intermittently throughout the night. A number of Trains heard and a great deal of Whistling & Banging going on, probably a relief going on. Signaled to enemy sent up people flare and at other times a green + also red but nothing appeared to follow. Weather Dull but Dry. | |
| | 13/8 | | Enemy shelled B 11 and B 12. Observation appeared to be done by enemy Aeroplane. At 11 pm our Transport at St JEAN was fired at with Shrapnel. Ypres received attention during the evening several Shells falling in the centre of the Town. Enemy Machine Guns fairly active during the night. A Patrol of 2nd R. Londons went out, a disused Trench was found at C29.93.4, was detonated and led the lad ready for storming. A number of enemy bombs were found, they was detonated and led the lad ready for storming. A Searchlight was observed on our left flank in a northerly direction. Enemy Aeroplanes during the day were very busy. Weather Dry. | |

Army Form C. 2118.

# WAR DIARY
## or
## INTELLIGENCE SUMMARY

*(Erase heading not required.)*

Instructions regarding War Diaries and Intelligence Summaries are contained in F. S. Regs., Part II. and the Staff Manual respectively. Title Pages will be prepared in manuscript.

| Place | Date 1916 | Hour | Summary of Events and Information | Remarks and references to Appendices |
|---|---|---|---|---|
| YPRES | August 14th | | Everything in our sector fairly Quiet, Enemy snipers too active. Our machine guns did a little during the morning & evening periods. Wind N of W. Wea<sup>r</sup>. | |
| | 15th | | Weather. Sunny. At 0830 two of our Aeroplanes attacked and forced down a German plane. It was not afterwards, but recovered & planed down towards enemy lines. It was obviously hit. Enemy artillery quiet, except for a little coast battery work. Our machine guns opened on a German working party during the night. 2 flares seen N<sup>o</sup> flying eastwards from German trenches. Two Officers from the Base arrived. Lieuts. ROWBOTHAM & STREET. Lights again very dull. | |
| | 16th | | Enemy artillery again very quiet. At 1400 B9 & B10 was shelled with whizz bangs. And again at 1630. Enemy fired Rifle Grenades at our right at about 12. Enemy retaliated with about 30 trench mortars, with little damage. Enemy medium Trench mortar bursts at our parapets throughout the night. One Officer reported from B'ce Lieut Robinson | |
| | | | LoSathe Somershot Brighter | |

Army Form C. 2118.

# WAR DIARY
## or
## INTELLIGENCE SUMMARY

(Erase heading not required.)

Instructions regarding War Diaries and Intelligence Summaries are contained in F. S. Regs., Part II. and the Staff Manual respectively. Title Pages will be prepared in manuscript.

| Place | Date 1916 | Hour | Summary of Events and Information | Remarks and references to Appendices |
|---|---|---|---|---|
| YPRES | 17th August | | Enemy Artillery Quiet along the whole front. Snipers very quiet. Our machine guns fired on enemy's communication trenches during the night. Two men were seen in front of our line at ODERHOUSE, 9 hours fired on them without result. Later a patrol was out but failed to find any trace of them. Weather Sunny. | |
| | 18th Aug. | | 10A.M. K.R.R. That Rauss Relieved Bn Bethoff 8 R/R gun machine guns with respect by the 87th Co. 5th Can. of 886 R.M.R. Relief Completed at 6am 19th. Enemy machine guns fired short bursts at infrequent intervals. 10.8 a.m. Still, Muggy, church during morning. | |
| | 19th Aug | | Enemy Artillery Shas a few H.E's at H.31 about 1300. An enemy patrol was seen about 01.45 30 yards from our line. They were fired upon without success. Weather Cloudy all day. Heavy showers in late evening. | |
| | 20th Aug | | 0A.M. 300 enemy dropped stello in the "bremontien" about machine guns guilt full Sell Fir Corner. Drew fires to H.5.B. A patrol by the K.O.S.B. returned through our lines bringing in H. 38225 German RJT. & some Bombs. | |

W. Cotter, Mich. H

Army Form C.2118.

# WAR DIARY
## INTELLIGENCE SUMMARY
*(Erase heading not required.)*

| Place | Date | Hour | Summary of Events and Information | Remarks and references to Appendices |
|---|---|---|---|---|
| YPRES | 21st Augt 1916 | | At 1500 a Bombardment of C.29 Central by our 4.5" Hows and T. Mortars was successfully carried out as per programme. During the night bursts of Shrapnel were fired on trenches made in forage. During the bombardment, Enemy Retaliation on the whole feeble. At 3015 a Klaxon horn and gongs were heard from direction of BOESINGHE, after 20 minutes the situation appeared normal. At 3330 the horn was again heard, on neither occasion was there any indications of Gas. No wind did not appear favourable for a Gas attack. W. Butts Brigade. Enemy artillery dropped H. Shells on HELL FIRE Corner during the afternoon and at 0815 about a dozen H.E. on Potijze. Machine Gun active at "Stand to" and "Stand down" — Enemy working party dispersed by Machine Gun fire. Cries were heard & no further work done outside parapet. Searchlight. 6 Rathe Chalosny. | 2nd Bn? |

# WAR DIARY or INTELLIGENCE SUMMARY

Army Form C. 2118.

(Erase heading not required.)

| Place | Date 1916 | Hour | Summary of Events and Information | Remarks and references to Appendices |
|---|---|---|---|---|
| YPRES | 24th August | | Lieut. DYER reported for duty as Transport Officer the day. Lieut. K.S. MacAlpin posted to command 19th Company, 4th Division. General situation quiet. Our Machine Guns fired on Enemy Communication trenches intermittently throughout the night. Louvres and covered Emplacement at F.S. Elephant Emplacement at WHITE CHATEAU fitted in ready for use. Roof being covered. | |
| | 25th August | | Weather fine. Situation quiet on Divisional front. Enemy Aeroplanes very busy. Our Machine Guns making steady shooting at them. | |
| | 26th August 27th – | | | |
| | 28th Aug | | The Company was relieved in the line by the 88th Brigade. Company returning by March Route to Camp at BRANDHOEK. | |
| | 29 August | | Company employed in cleaning & overhauling Guns & Equipment. Exchanging men's clothing. General clean up. | |

Army Form C. 2118.

# WAR DIARY
## or
## INTELLIGENCE SUMMARY

*(Erase heading not required.)*

Instructions regarding War Diaries and Intelligence Summaries are contained in F. S. Regs., Part II. and the Staff Manual respectively. Title Pages will be prepared in manuscript.

| Place | Date 1916 | Hour | Summary of Events and Information | Remarks and references to Appendices |
|---|---|---|---|---|
| BRANDHOEK | 30th Aug | | Physical, Running & Arms Drill combined with Gun Instruction and cleaning Camp Lines carried out. Lecture by C.O. Subject: Elevating & Traversing Dials. to Sections, Gun Instruction. N.C.O's Strappy & Drill Gun Instruction, One section on the Range, Lecture to | |
| | 31st Aug | | N.C.O's Subject: Range Cards & other tui. Weather fine. Lieut McLean joined the Coy from 168 M.G.Co. Strength of Company:— Officers = 8 O.R's = 146 | |

Edward Greyhurst Captain
Comdg 86 Co. Machine Gun Corps

29th Division.
86th Infantry Brigade.
-------

86th BRIGADE

MACHINE GUN COMPANY

SEPTEMBER 1 9 1 6

Vol 7

War Diary.
— of —
86th Company. Machine Gun Corps.
— Vol: 7. —
From 1st September to 30th Sept
— 1916. —

Army Form C. 2118.

# WAR DIARY
## INTELLIGENCE SUMMARY

Instructions regarding War Diaries and Intelligence Summaries are contained in F.S. Regs., Part II. and the Staff Manual respectively. Title Pages will be prepared in manuscript.

No. 240 Coy 1st Bn. Machine Gun Corps (Y.M.)

| Place | Date | Hour | Summary of Events and Information | Remarks and references to Appendices |
|---|---|---|---|---|
| Brandhoek (or Splinter) | 13/8/16 | | The Company are in Divisional Reserve and are employed in digging & instructing, also finding out working party all day. Bathing, Refitting & General Duties. Making the approaches to C.T. from 2nd to 1st Line on right of the Canal. C. Section M. Muncken Farm. Competition & Shoot together with a Great Yser H.Q. & H.Q. Sec. Run on 11/8/16. All ranks enjoyed great keenness. The entries to St Jean, the Company relieved the following Guns: Company in the Left Brigade Sector. N Jean state No.6: Open & Welague Farm & the White Château — L. Glass == 2 in St. Muncken Farm. == St Jean Jean. 2 in == 2 in Reeks Roundabout and Duffy == Poitize Sector. 1 Gun to Aasif Salient for Ou Bof. 2 Guns in Support on the Ypres Canal North Bank Company West. | |
| | 14/16 | | (Maintz) O War Office Emplacement at Prowse Farm in Saint Chartier continued work. Also on 6th English Farm MG section on Beehan Farm = lean Montcure in Out Guest just 8 taking all cambers N.E. Guns salved as follows. YPRES Canal X.1.C. 70.1 / Raiperes X.7.0.95.1 1 AG. C. 27.C.95.10. 2 on St Julier Road Zillebeke marsh | |

2348 Wt. W1522/869 750,000 1/18 J.B.C. & A. Forms/C.2118/22.

Army Form C. 2118.

# WAR DIARY
## or
## INTELLIGENCE SUMMARY.
(Erase heading not required.)

Instructions regarding War Diaries and Intelligence Summaries are contained in F. S. Regs., Part II. and the Staff Manual respectively. Title pages will be prepared in manuscript.

| Place | Date | Hour | Summary of Events and Information | Remarks and references to Appendices |
|---|---|---|---|---|
| YPRES | 9th Sept. 1916 | | A machine gun at C.29.a.2.8. was fired upon by our Artillery. The gun did not again fire. For the last two nights a hostile machine gun has been worrying our Infantry by shooting down the ST JEAN – YPRES ROAD. A small retaliation scheme was arranged yesterday afternoon to cope with this gun. This was carried out about 2.15 (when the M/Gs opened fire) and was entirely successful. The hostile fire ceased and did not open again until 0115, when two bursts were fired by us. This silenced the machine gun and it did not fire again. Th Coxen's emplacements at PROWSE FARM was continued also at ENGLISH Farm. Weather Sunny. | |
| | 10th Sept | | Enemy Artillery quiet on the whole. Machine guns quiet during the day, but active on both sides during the night. Snipers quiet, probably owing to bad light. Weather. Warm & Dry. | |
| | 11th Sept | | Enemy Artillery showed normal activity. He shelled ST JEAN from 1600 – 1800 with 77m.m. and 4.2 Hows. Our 18pdr. retaliated slightly. | |

Army Form C. 2118.

# WAR DIARY
## or
## INTELLIGENCE SUMMARY.
*(Erase heading not required.)*

Instructions regarding War Diaries and Intelligence Summaries are contained in F. S. Regs., Part II. and the Staff Manual respectively. Title pages will be prepared in manuscript.

| Place | Date | Hour | Summary of Events and Information | Remarks and references to Appendices |
|---|---|---|---|---|
| YPRES | 11th Sept. 1916 | | Between 2045 and 2330, our Arty. retaliated on three active machine guns which were gradually silenced, one of them near WELL COTTAGE being particularly persistent. Enemy machine guns active during the night opposite R Battalion and on the L. flank of L. Battalion. Several patrols went out, nothing unusual to report. Lieutenant K.M. MOIR joined the Company this day from the Machine Gun Corps Base. Weather. Dull & Dry. | |
| | 12th Sept. | | Enemy Artillery opposite our right Divisional front was rather more active than usual. But on the left it was very quiet. Enemy fired about 20 rounds into POTIJZE WOOD several of the shells failed to explode. No damage done to our emplacements. Enemy Machine Guns on the whole quiet. Snipers active both day and night. Pigeons seen flying from behind our lines to enemy lines. Weather. Showery. | |

Army Form C. 2118.

# WAR DIARY
## or
## INTELLIGENCE SUMMARY.
(Erase heading not required.)

Instructions regarding War Diaries and Intelligence Summaries are contained in F. S. Regs., Part II. and the Staff Manual respectively. Title pages will be prepared in manuscript.

| Place | Date 1916 | Hour | Summary of Events and Information | Remarks and references to Appendices |
|---|---|---|---|---|
| YPRES | 13 Sept. | | Enemy artillery Quiet. Machine Guns quiet during the day; slight activity during the night. Snipers active during the morning, quieter later. One German Signaller "stood out" with a helmet after one of our Sniper Shots. Several of our Patrols went out, they reported the usual work activity. One patrol brought back 3 bombs of the usual type (stick) and buttons with the figure 5 on them. Pigeons seen flying from enemy lines and from Rear of our lines towards enemy(?). Weather: Rain during morning, dry remainder of day. The Battalions in our Brigade Sector were relieved by the Battalions in Support 16th Middlesex relieved 2nd Royal Fusiliers, 1st Lancashire Fusiliers relieved 2nd Royal Fusiliers. The relief went through without incident. Enemy Artillery Quiet on the whole. Machine Guns active from Dawn "Stand to" till Daylight. | |
| | 14th Sept. | | | |

Army Form C. 2118.

# WAR DIARY
## or
## INTELLIGENCE SUMMARY.
(Erase heading not required.)

| Place | Date | Hour | Summary of Events and Information | Remarks and references to Appendices |
|---|---|---|---|---|
| YPRES | 1916. | | | |
| | 14th Sept | | Snipers Quiet. | |
| | | | A Patrol went out from our line in front of A 76 A 5 from 24.00 - | |
| | | 02.00 | They reported no Enemy patrols or working parties heard. Enemy very quiet, and his line appeared to be thinly held. | |
| | | | Pigeons passed over R.F.A. 8 and settled behind German front line. | |
| | | | Weather. Heavy rain. Dull & misty. | |
| | 15th Sept | | Enemy Artillery Quiet during the day. | |
| | | 23.00 | after discharge of Gas by us. Our Artillery and Machine Guns kept up a heavy fire for one hour and a quarter, with occasional bursts later. Enemy retaliation on the whole feeble, especially with Artillery. Most of the retaliation was by Trench Mortars. Some damage done in B.9. and 5 men buried, but more were seriously hurt. | |
| | | | Enemy Machine Guns normal. Action at "Stand to". | |
| | | | A considerable number of Rockets went up from the German lines on our Gas discharge but were observed in the "Gassed" area. | |
| | | | No horns or Pound alarms were heard. | |

Army Form C. 2118.

# WAR DIARY
## or
## INTELLIGENCE SUMMARY.
(Erase heading not required.)

Instructions regarding War Diaries and Intelligence Summaries are contained in F. S. Regs., Part II. and the Staff Manual respectively. Title pages will be prepared in manuscript.

| Place | Date | Hour | Summary of Events and Information | Remarks and references to Appendices |
|---|---|---|---|---|
| | 1916 | | | |
| YPRES | 15th Sept. | | At 24.00 two patrols went out to observe, if possible, the results of the Gas. The first was attacked by a wiring party, and withdrew to own trenches. | |
| | | | The second reported conditions in German line normal. | |
| | | | At 16.30 5 Pigeons went per R. Sector to Enemy's lines from direction of POTIJZE. | |
| | 16th Sept. | | Weather: Very dull, Showers during late evening & night. | |
| | | | Four Aeroplane emplacement were built and a new pattern Aeroplane mounting erected. It is a useful and practical mounting suitable for both Vickers and LEWIS guns. | |
| | | | Enemy Artillery was Quiet on our R. Sector his Machine Guns were active during the Evening "Stand to" but on the L. Sector they were abnormally Quiet. | |
| | | | Our Machine Guns during the night fired on Gaps in the enemy's wire and on to communications. | |
| | | | Weather: Dry & Sunny. | |

Army Form C. 2118.

# WAR DIARY
## or
## INTELLIGENCE SUMMARY.
(Erase heading not required.)

Instructions regarding War Diaries and Intelligence Summaries are contained in F.S. Regs., Part II. and the Staff Manual respectively. Title pages will be prepared in manuscript.

| Place | Date | Hour | Summary of Events and Information | Remarks and references to Appendices |
|---|---|---|---|---|
| YPRES | 1915 | | | |
| | 17th Sept. | | Enemy Artillery Quiet on the whole of our Front, a few shells dropped on CAVAN TRENCH and on B.9. but little damage was done. There was heavy shelling this morning to the South from 0900 to 0930 about RAIL-WAY WOOD. Machine Guns Quiet, one at C.19.d.4.5. was attacked by M.G. with Rifle Grenades from A.6. There was some retaliation with Rifle Grenades, but the Gun did not fire again. Ustalks. Bright & Clear. | |
| | 18th Sept. | | Enemy Artillery on the whole Quiet, about 1500 they dropped 10 shells about 25 yards behind X.4. Our Artillery silenced M/Guns on the L. Sector. Enemy Machine Guns on the R. Sector active during the night. Quiet otherwise. One of our Patrols encountered an enemy working party at the MOUND they were working very hurried and retired to their trenches after about 2 hours. Our Machine Guns were relieved by the 87th Co. and we in turn relieved the 88th Co. on the Right. The relief passed off without incident & Weather. Heavy Rain practically all day. | |

Army Form C. 2118.

# WAR DIARY
## or
## INTELLIGENCE SUMMARY.

(Erase heading not required.)

Instructions regarding War Diaries and Intelligence Summaries are contained in F. S. Regs., Part II. and the Staff Manual respectively. Title pages will be prepared in manuscript.

| Place | Date | Hour | Summary of Events and Information | Remarks and references to Appendices |
|---|---|---|---|---|
| YPRES | 1915 | | | |
| | 19th Sept | | Day very Quiet, nothing of incident occurring. Weather:- Heavy Showers | |
| | 20th Sept | | In the R. Sector the enemy Artillery showed slightly increased activity. In the L. it was very Quiet. Work going on along the whole front all night opposite R. Sector, the enemy making a considerable amount of noise. Weather Showery and Cold. | |
| | 21st Sept | | Enemy Artillery Quiet on the whole, about 1700 four of our own Shells dropped behind our line, H.E and I Shrapnel. Enemy Machine Guns Quiet during the day, active at night. Our Aeroplanes were very active at 1230 one of them brought down an observation Balloon by Rocket fire. At 18.30 one of ours went over enemy lines, heavily fired upon. When over enemy's front line, he dived, the fire ceased and he emptied his Machine Gun into the Trench, returning unmolested. Weather, Showery & very Cold. Captain Ja Lyppu rejoined from Hospital | |

T2134. Wt. W708-776. 500000. 4/15. Sir J. C. & S.

Army Form C. 2118.

# WAR DIARY
or
INTELLIGENCE SUMMARY.
(Erase heading not required.)

Instructions regarding War Diaries and Intelligence Summaries are contained in F. S. Regs., Part II. and the Staff Manual respectively. Title pages will be prepared in manuscript.

| Place | Date | Hour | Summary of Events and Information | Remarks and references to Appendices |
|---|---|---|---|---|
| YPRES | 1915 | | | |
| | 22nd Sept. | | Enemy Artillery more active on our L. sub Sector shelling the Reserve and Support trenches. Machine Guns active during the night. Weather: Clear & warm. | |
| | 23rd Sept. | | Enemy Artillery very quiet. There was no retaliation in any form for the shelling at night. Machine Guns very quiet. Contact aeroplanes @ WHITE CHATEAU Completed and ready for occupation. Weather: Misty early morning later Bright and Sunny. | |
| | 24th Sept. | | Enemy artillery very quiet on the whole. Retaliated slightly for our shelling, batw. 2nd. 1530 – 1830, on Crater N°3 and its junction to the Trench. Machine Guns active as "stand to" and during the night. At 1030 two hostile Aeroplanes attempted to cross over, but were driven back by our A.A. Guns. | |

**Army Form C. 2118.**

# WAR DIARY
## OR
## INTELLIGENCE SUMMARY.
*(Erase heading not required.)*

| Place | Date | Hour | Summary of Events and Information | Remarks and references to Appendices |
|---|---|---|---|---|
| YPRES | 1916 | | | |
| | 24th Sept | | Our Artillery fired with success on several hostile working parties and on the work at several points. Upon one of our Patrols opening fire on a working party, the enemy retaliated with Machine gun fire. Weather Sunny. | |
| | 25th Sept | | Enemy Artillery quiet on the whole. Two or three large shells in the direction of MUD LANE towards evening and a few light ones on POTIJZE WOOD. Machine Guns quiet all day. Very occasional bursts of fire at night. A Standing Patrol in Crater No 6 reports metallic noises in enemy's lines, possibly gas cylinders. At 0800 an enemy Aeroplane flying low was hunted back ow its lines by two of our Machines. She was fired upon by our LEWIS GUNS, but dropped Star Lights, which were H.E. and Shrapnel on RAILWAY FARM. Weather Bright. Clear day | |

Army Form C. 2118.

# WAR DIARY
## or
## INTELLIGENCE SUMMARY.
(Erase heading not required.)

Instructions regarding War Diaries and Intelligence Summaries are contained in F. S. Regs., Part II. and the Staff Manual respectively. Title pages will be prepared in manuscript.

| Place | Date | Hour | Summary of Events and Information | Remarks and references to Appendices |
|---|---|---|---|---|
| YPRES. | 19/6 | | | |
| | 26th Sept. | | Enemy activity was very slight consisting chiefly of mild and scattered T.M. Bombardments that were promptly silenced by retaliation. | |
| | | | An enemy working party at the MOUND was dispersed by our Bombers firing Rifle Grenades. | |
| | | | Weather - Sunny. | |
| | 27th Sept. | | Enemy Artillery Slight also their Machine Guns. | |
| | | | A few gas shells were noted. | |
| | | | Hostile Aircraft made some small abrupt activity. | |
| | | | Our Patrols were active throughout the night. One patrol located an enemy wiring party about I.12.a.3.4. The patrol took cover in shell holes and directed Lewis gun fire on the party who hurriedly withdrew. At 22.45 the party attempted to resume their work but were again dispersed by fire, apparently some were hit as cries were heard. | |
| | | | Our Bombers also threw Bombs. | |
| | | | Weather, Windy & Showery later.  Lieut Laver gone to 17/6 | |

# WAR DIARY
or
## INTELLIGENCE SUMMARY.
(Erase heading not required.)

Army Form C. 2118.

| Place | Date | Hour | Summary of Events and Information | Remarks and references to Appendices |
|---|---|---|---|---|
| | 1916 | | | |
| YPRES | 28th Sept | | The Day was Quiet throughout. 3 p.m. The King of the Belgians accompanied by Prince Arthur of Teck and the Corps Commander (Sir. A. Hunter-Weston) visited the trenches and expressed his high appreciation of all he saw. The Company was relieved in the line by the 88th Brigade. He relief passed off without event. The Company returned to Billets at BRANDHOEK together. Rain. Some rain. | |
| BRANDHOEK | 29th Sept | | The Company was overhauled overhauling the Gun Equipment and also the men were Bathed. Weather unsettled. | |
| | 30th Sept | | Drill, Machine Gun instruction and lectures was carried out. Weather fine. | |
| | | | Signed E.B. Hicks. Issued from the 2 Lieut Hrs Bros Acting Adjutant 86th Machine Gun Corps. Comdg 86th Machine Gun Corps. | |

29th Division.

86th Infantry Brigade.

----------

86th BRIGADE

MACHINE GUN COMPANY

OCTOBER 1 9 1 6

Operation Orders attached.

Vol 9

Confidential

War Diary
of
86th Company. Machine Gun Corps.

From October 1st to October 31st 1916.

Volume 8.

# WAR DIARY
## or
## INTELLIGENCE SUMMARY.

Army Form C. 2118.

VOL. VIII

| Place | Date | Hour | Summary of Events and Information | Remarks and references to Appendices |
|---|---|---|---|---|
| BRANDHOEK | 1st October 1916 | | Drill & Gun Instruction carried out. | |
| | 2nd Oct. | | The Coys Commander (Capt Sir Alfred Hickman Bart) inspected the Company & Camp. The Davies taken Prison of War 1st July 16 now reported "Died of Wounds" previously reported Wounded & Missing. Lieut. Rose Lewkam posted to 61st Company as a Transport Officer. The Company was inspected by the Corps Commander who had 61 some (to C.) good life than leaving to go South. | |
| | 3rd Oct | | Weather Intermittent Rain. | |
| | 4th Oct | | The Camp at Brandhoek was taken over by the 164 M.G. Co. 55th Division. The Company entrained at the CHEESE MARKET POPERINGHE 3.30pm arriving at WORMHOUDT about 6.30pm. Then marched to Billets at HERZEELE. Sergt. Roonan having been sent on earlier as Billeting N.C.O. Lieut OREPEN and Sergt McDougall were sent on to D HOURS for Billeting purposes. | |
| | | | Weather: Heavy showers. | |

Army Form C. 2118.

# WAR DIARY
## or
## INTELLIGENCE SUMMARY.
*(Erase heading not required.)*

Instructions regarding War Diaries and Intelligence Summaries are contained in F. S. Regs., Part II. and the Staff Manual respectively. Title pages will be prepared in manuscript.

| Place | Date | Hour | Summary of Events and Information | Remarks and references to Appendices |
|---|---|---|---|---|
| | 1916 | | | |
| HERZEELE | 4th Oct. | | Drill, Gun Instruction & overhauling of SAA carried out. Waters works KO | |
| | 5th Oct. | | Drill, Gun Instruction carried out. Baths unearthed | |
| | 6th Oct. | | Co assos, Works Pty &c | |
| | 7th Oct. | | Moved by march route to WORMHOUDT. entrained at 9.30 p.m. | |
| | | | for PROVEN | |
| | 8th Oct. | | ENTRAINED at PROVEN for SALEUX arrived about 8 p.m. moved | |
| | | | by march Route to DAOURS. arriving about 4 a.m. 9th inst | |
| DAOURS | 9th Oct | | The Company was rested | |
| | 10th Oct | | The Company moved by march route to DERNACOURT via LONGUEVILLE | |
| | | | - BONNY - HEILLY - BOIRE arriving about 4 p.m. Weather fine. | |
| BERNACOURT | 11th Oct | | DRILL & Gun Instruction. Officers went out to recoonoitre the | |
| | | | Road to LONGUEVILLE. Information being received that the Division will | |
| | | | take over line between THILLOY and GAUDECOURT. | |
| | 12th Oct | | Drill & Gun Instruction. Instructions received to more | |
| | | | to MAMETZ WOOD 13th inst. | |
| | | | Weather Dry | |

# WAR DIARY or INTELLIGENCE SUMMARY

Army Form C. 2118.

| Place | Date | Hour | Summary of Events and Information | Remarks and references to Appendices |
|---|---|---|---|---|
| MAMETZ WOOD | 1916 13th Oct. | | Battalion moved by march route to Mametz Wood arriving about 2 pm, thence went into Bivouac, preparing to move up tomorrow to the vicinity of FLERS and GUEDACOURT. The Germans have been slightly less active than usual today, but the shelling increases towards evening. Weather fine. | |
| | 14th Oct | | Situation unchanged. 3 German aeroplanes this morning flew low over our front trenches and attempted to fire with machine guns. Our artillery has been active this afternoon but met with little response from the enemy. FLERS and our front trenches, however, received some attention at intervals during the day. | |

Army Form C. 2118.

# WAR DIARY
## or
## INTELLIGENCE SUMMARY.
(Erase heading not required.)

Instructions regarding War Diaries and Intelligence Summaries are contained in F. S. Regs., Part II. and the Staff Manual respectively. Title pages will be prepared in manuscript.

| Place | Date | Hour | Summary of Events and Information | Remarks and references to Appendices |
|---|---|---|---|---|
| | 1916 | | | |
| MAMETZ | 15/16 Oct | | Situation on our Corps front unchanged. Our Artillery has been active throughout the day. The enemy replied by intermittently shelling our front line trenches and FLERS, DE Valley E. of FLERS was shelled with lachrymatory shells. LONGUEVAL was shelled from direction of BAPAUME. Weather dull & cloudy. | |
| | 16th Oct. | | Situation unchanged. Enemy Activity. Between 11.30 and 12.30 FLERS was shelled with heavy H.E. and Bulls Road was shelled with 5.9" GIRD and GIRD SUPPORT were shelled intermittently throughout the day. Our artillery has been active throughout the day. Weather, Overcast & much Rain. | |
| | 17th Oct. | | Our Artillery has shown its usual activity today. German Aeroplanes again attempted this morning to open fire on our troops with machine Guns, but so far as we know, did no damage. Another Aeroplane dropped some bombs in the vicinity of VIVIER MILL with no result | |

# WAR DIARY
## or
## INTELLIGENCE SUMMARY.

**Army Form C. 2118.**

| Place | Date | Hour | Summary of Events and Information | Remarks and references to Appendices |
|---|---|---|---|---|
| | 1916 | | | |
| MAMETZ | 17th OCT | | FLERS was shelled with 15c.m. in the morning and GUEUDCOURT was heavily shelled for a quarter of an hour, about 1600. During the afternoon parties carrying wounded were seen going in the direction of VILLERS-AU-FLOS Church. Weather Sunny. Very Frosty Night. | |
| | 18th OCT | | No 20922. Corporal B. Fletcher sent to the Base as an Instructor. The Right division advanced its line 500yards on a frontage of 750yards, capturing 00/R 100prisoners. A "TANK" was in action 25 minutes in the German Trenches and did great execution among the enemy before returning to our trenches. Hostile Aeroplanes were active over the Back areas Yesterday afternoon. White lights were dropped when over the Quarry and SWITCH TRENCH. Weather - Very Misty most Thing - rain during the Evening & Night. Situation unchanged. The Germans Opposite our Left Division were evidently very nervous. | |
| | 19th OCT | | | |

Army Form C. 2118.

# WAR DIARY
## of
## INTELLIGENCE SUMMARY.
(Erase heading not required.)

Instructions regarding War Diaries and Intelligence Summaries are contained in F. S. Regs., Part II. and the Staff Manual respectively. Title pages will be prepared in manuscript.

| Place | Date | Hour | Summary of Events and Information | Remarks and references to Appendices |
|---|---|---|---|---|
| MAMETZ | 19th Oct | | Continued this morning as a number of red rockets were sent up followed by a heavy barrage over our front Trenches which lasted for 25 minutes. A considerable amount of movement of men and Transport was observed in H.2. central and H.3. This was shelled with good effect by the captured 7.7 c.m. Gun. The Company moved over & relieved the 25th Company in their line. The exchange being carried out without incident. Weather: Very heavy rain and cold frosty night. | |
| FLERS | 20th Oct | | No change in the General situation. Hostile retaliation to our Artillery was about normal during the day, there has been much Aeroplane activity on both sides. Night Quiet except at 0515 relief WRR Rellies heavily from BAPAUME. Neither Colo Ramo Transport and Orderly room moved to POMMIERS REDOUBT. | |
| | 21st Oct | | Worthless between 1630 and 1730 Aus and Intense Barrage | |

Army Form C. 2118.

# WAR DIARY
## or
## INTELLIGENCE SUMMARY.
(Erase heading not required.)

Instructions regarding War Diaries and Intelligence Summaries are contained in F. S. Regs., Part II. and the Staff Manual respectively. Title pages will be prepared in manuscript.

| Place | Date | Hour | Summary of Events and Information | Remarks and references to Appendices |
|---|---|---|---|---|
| | 1916 | | Continued | |
| FLERS | 2nd Oct | | was put up by the enemy on the LES BOEUFS sector. DEVILLE Valley and the Quarry in S.12.b. were shelled with 15.c.m. and 21.c.m. from 0930 to 1900, the deliberate fire never ceased for more than 10 minutes at a time. | |
| | | | A great deal of the enemy's front is now wired. | |
| | | | A hostile machine gun is trained on our new trench N.20.c.8.8. | |
| | | | Our Artillery active throughout the day. | |
| | | | Weather fair. Very cold. | |
| | 3rd Oct | | Artillery – Hostile activity was about normal, between 0800 and 1600, after that normal. 20 Batteries were engaged, four emplacements were destroyed and three damaged. | |
| | | | A great deal of Aerial activity on both sides. Two hostile Machines were brought down as the results of combats. Our planes dropped bombs on THILLOY. | |
| | | | Conclusive evidence has been discovered that explosive bullets were used by the Germans in the vicinity of THIEPVAL, about 500 rounds of the ammunition being discovered by the | |

# WAR DIARY or INTELLIGENCE SUMMARY

Army Form C. 2118.

| Place | Date | Hour | Summary of Events and Information | Remarks and references to Appendices |
|---|---|---|---|---|
| FLERS | 1916 22nd Oct | | Casualties in action 9 O.R. killed. 3 O.R. wounded and 1 O.R. missing. Enemy Artillery normal. Our own Kepping up a steady fire through out the day. Weather, cold, frosty air. | |
| | 23rd Oct | | Operation orders issued for attack on the German Trenches to take place 7th inst. Copy of Company orders attached. Large numbers of our Aeroplanes up during the day observing Bombardment proceeding our Right. Hers came in for a good deal of shelling during the afternoon. Weather, slightly warmer. | |
| | 24th/Oct | | Operations postponed 24 hours will now take place on the 25th instant. The following promotions and appointments, were made in the Company. 1021004 T/Sgt J. Doyle. J. Promoted Sergt. 20973 Corporal McNutt appointed Lance Sergt. 20934 L/Cpl George C. promoted Corp. 30580 L/Cpl Lawson J. appts. acty Corporal 30983 L/Cpl Coleman W. to recur pay of Appointment. acty Cpl Byars to Corporal. Weather: Heavy Rain. See Signature | |

# WAR DIARY or INTELLIGENCE SUMMARY.

Army Form C. 2118.

| Place | Date | Hour | Summary of Events and Information | Remarks and references to Appendices |
|---|---|---|---|---|
| FIERS | 1916 | | | |
| | 26th Oct | | 2n Ashby Killed Acha. Meade. Heavy Rain. Cold. Work in the trenches much impeded by the bad weather. | |
| | 27th Oct | | Continued Bombardment continuing on both sides. Weather. Cold + rainy. The operations referred to have now been postponed till October 28th. | |
| | 28th Oct | | Operations again postponed again until 1st November 1916. Weather wet. | |
| | 29th Oct | | at 6.00 Yesterday there was a heavy bombardment on our right + left. This sector did not receive much bombardment. | |
| | | | Warhalwt - Orders received to move out tomorrow. Relieved in the line by the 1st Australian Infantry Brigade | |
| | 30th Oct | | The relief was completed by 8.30pm. The Company then returned to Bivouacs at Trench wood. Heavy Rain | |

T2134. Wt. W708-776. 500000. 4/15. Sir J.C. & S.

Army Form C. 2118.

# WAR DIARY
## or
## INTELLIGENCE SUMMARY.
*(Erase heading not required.)*

| Place | Date | Hour | Summary of Events and Information | Remarks and references to Appendices |
|---|---|---|---|---|
| | | 1916 | | |
| VILLE Sur Ancre | 31.10.16 | at 6pm | The Company moved on march Route from Mametz to Ville around at 6pm. Billets were provided. Very Heavy Rain throughout the day | |

31.10.16

[signature]
Comdg 86 Co Machine Gun Corps

Operation Order No. 16
by Major R. Beckwith M.C. Comdg 86th Company
Machine Gun Corps

23rd October 1916

Reference Map:
57c. S.W. 1/20,000 &
Trench Diagram No 3 1/Oct, 20th 1/10000.

General    1.    The XV Corps will continue the attack on
Information      October ___ at an hour ZERO which will be notified
                 later.    The 8th Australian Brigade, 5th Div.
                 will be on the left of the 86th Brigade, and the
                 87th Bde on the right.

Objective  2.    The Brigade will assault (a) BAYONET
                 TRENCH and consolidate it. (b) BACON TRENCH
                 and from there move forward and dig in as
                 close as possible to BARLEY TRENCH.

Plan of    3.    Battalions will attack with four
Attack           companies in line of company column
                 i.e. in four waves.    During the night
                 of the 24th Battalions will be formed up in the
                 forward lines and shell holes well closed
                 up in the above order.    The German trenches
                 will be subjected to a slow preliminary bomb
                 -ardment until ZERO. There will be no
                 intense bombardment before that hour.
                 Artillery programme later.

                     At ZERO hour a heavy artillery barrage
                 will open over a zone of about 150 yards on
                 either side of BAYONET TRENCH.

                     Immediately this barrage opens the
                 attack will move forward with obj———
                 BAYONET TRENCH.    Having captured
                 BAYONET TRENCH there will be a pause of 20 minutes
                 the whole

**Plan of Attack continued**

The whole attack will re-organise and move forward to the second objective.

The advance to BACON TRENCH will be in the same order, attack moving forward with the barrage.

**2nd Objective**

4. The dividing line between the 86th and 87th Bdes will be N.20.a.1.99 — N.19.b.8.3 FACTORY CORNER

The dividing line between the 86th & 87th Bdes will be N.20.b.99.61. — N.20.d.3.4. — N.20.c.8.1. — T.1.b.3.1.

The dividing line between 2nd Royal Fusiliers and 1st Lanc't. Fusiliers will be N.20.b.6.9 — N.20.a.15.00.

**Assembly for Attack**

The 86th Bde will be formed up as follows:—

1st Lancashire Fusiliers — Right Sub-sector from N.20.c.50.60 to N.20.c.8.1.

2nd Royal Fusiliers — Left Sub-sector from N.20.c.50.60 to N.19.b.8.3.

1st Royal Dublin Fus'rs. — SWIFT TRENCH
16th Middlesex Regt. — DELVILLE WOOD

**Machine Guns**

5. At the ZERO hour 8 guns will open a heavy barrage along BARLEY TRENCH continuing this until BAYONET TRENCH is captured. During the forward advance of the Infantry from BAYONET TRENCH these guns will continue on BARLEY TRENCH until their fire is masked. 8 guns will open along BACON TRENCH in the same manner.

Before ZERO 8 guns will take up forward positions in No Man's Land their

their special task will be to deal with hostile machine gun fire as soon as Infantry advance.

When BAYONET TRENCH is occupied 2 of these guns will move forward to it and take up positions there; the other two will move forward with the fourth wave of advance and take up positions in BACON TRENCH. As soon as the situation admits, another 4 guns will be moved forward to BAYONET TRENCH.

**STOKES MORTARS**

6. Before ZERO hour four STOKES guns will take up positions as far forward in NO MANS LAND as possible with 50 rounds per gun, prepared to open fire on any hostile machine guns in range.

These guns will move into BAYONET TRENCH when this is captured. In the further advance from BAYONET TRENCH these four guns will follow the Infantry: two on either flank.

**GUN DETAIL**

7. No. 3 section under Lieuts MOIR & DOFFY with their guns in pairs will move out before ZERO to shell holes as far forward as possible to BAYONET TRENCH. When this trench is occupied 2 guns under Lt DOFFY will move into and occupy positions in the trench.

2 guns under Lt MOIR will move forward with the 4th wave of Infantry and take up positions in BACON TRENCH.

No. 1. section under Lieuts. MACLEAN & ORPEN will occupy positions in the LEFT forward SECTOR.

No. 2. section under Lieut. STREET will occupy positions in the RIGHT forward SECTOR. As soon as the situation permits 2 guns of No. 1 section and 2 guns of No. 2 section will be sent forward (under an officer if possible) to take up positions in BAYONET TRENCH. These 8 guns will open a heavy barrage on BARLEY TRENCH (see para 8)

No. 4 section under Captain P.A. BYRNE and Lieut. FLETCHER will occupy a gun position vicinity of N.25.d.8.3. These guns will open on BACON TRENCH (see para 5 (b))

RECON-
NAISSANCE    8. Officers commanding sections must make a thorough reconnaissance of the positions, work out their ranges, direction and elevation, and thoroughly explain to all ranks the operation.

CO-ORDINATES
of
OBJECTIVES    9. 

| | | |
|---|---|---|
| BAYONET TRENCH | N. 20. c. 3. 9. | TO |
| | N. 20. d. 8. 1. | |
| BACON TRENCH | N. 21. d. 2. 5. | TO |
| | N. 21. a. 0. 5. | |
| BARLEY TRENCH | N. 21. b. 3. 5. | TO |
| | N. 15. c. 7. 9. | |

AMMUNITION
and WATER
DUMPS.    10. Two dumps will be established in the forward sectors and a man will be placed in charge. Ammunition carriers must be acquainted with their positions.

MISCELLAN.    11. The following points must be looked to by all officers and N.C.O's:-
(a) Positions of S.A. Ammunition and water dumps
(b) Spare parts, oil, Safety angles.
Watches will be synchronised at 7 P.M. 24th inst.
Supply of rations.

CASUALTIES    12. All casualties must be rendered as early as circumstances permit, giving Regtl. number, rank and name, nature of casualty. i.e.
  Killed
  Wounded
  Missing
  Prisoner of War
Making as certain as possible the nature of the casualty.

23/10/16.    86th Coy. Machine Gun Corps

In continuation of Operation Order
No. 16. of 23rd October 1916.

The following amendment will be made.
Para. 7 is cancelled and will read:-

2 guns of "A" Section under Captain
F.A. BYRNE will accompany the left flank of the
2nd Royal Fusiliers and assist in covering the advance
of the 8th Australian Brigade, finally establishing
at N.W.c.45.40. and N.W.c.60.60.

2 guns of "B" Section under Lieut. E.B.
FLETCHER will occupy the gun pits at N.20.d.3.5.
bringing enfilade fire to bear on BAYONET TRENCH.

As soon as the Trench is occupied by our
troops, these two guns will establish themselves in
BAYONET TRENCH and cover the advance of our
troops on to BACON TRENCH.

ADDITIONAL ORDERS 13. Two guns of the 24th M.Gun Coy. will occupy
positions in GIRD TRENCH and will assist in their
advance on BARLEY TRENCH from ZERO until
our advanced troops have consolidated in
their last objective (para 2).

EQUIPMENT 14. All ranks will wear skeleton
marching order and entrenching tool.
Box respirator. 2 sand bags per man.
    No. 1. Gun + Light Tripod
     " 2. Heavy Tripod
     " 3. 2 Belt Boxes + condenser
     " 4. Spare parts + 1 Belt Box
     " 5. Water + 1 Belt Box
     " 6. 2 Belt Boxes + 1st Aid case
    N.C.O. 2 Belt Boxes
Water bottles must be filled and 2 days rations
carried. Each man will carry two bombs.

Prisoners. 15. Prisoners will be sent back under a[n armed] escort to advanced cage at LONGUEVAL.

If handed over to Infantry a receipt should be taken. As far as possible prisoners should be handed over, and not taken back by gunners.

DIARIES. 16. All officers and N.C.Os will carry note books and pencils, diaries will be kept and handed in on conclusion of operations.

Reports should be sent back to Company Headquarters as frequently as circumstances permit.

Recognition of Ground occupied by our troops. 17. Aeroplane contact patrol will be up and flares will be let off in our forward positions, our contact planes answering by means of their Klaxon Horn or Very lights.

Artillery boards will at once be moved forward to behind the Parados of our forward positions.

HEADQUARTERS. 18. Brigade, Battalion and M.G. Gun Company Headquarters will not move.

H. W. Johnson 2/Lieut. & Adjt.
86th Coy. Machine Gun Corps

Copy No. 14

88th M.G. Co.

## 86th Bde Machine Gun Co.
## Operation Order.

Reference 1/20,000 57 D. S.E.
1/10,000 Trench map Sheet 57.D.SE.
Beaumont (1 and 2 parts)

The 29th Division is to take part in an attack on the enemy's trenches, on a date to be notified later, which will be indicated in these orders by the letter "Z".

**1. Objective of 86th Brigade.**

The area allotted to the 86th Brigade is:-
Northern Boundary:- Q.5.c.2.8. to Q.6.c.5.4.
Southern " :- Q.10.d.6.8. to Q.12.b.7.5.

**2. Location of Guns U.V.W.X & Y. day**

| Positions | No. | Commander |
|---|---|---|
| Bowery | 2 | Lt. J.F.B. Stevenson |
| Pilk Street | 1 } | " W. Milne |
| Essex Street | 1 } | |
| Newtownards | 1 } | " D.J.P. Duffy |
| "F" Street | 1 } | |

**3. "Z" day**

At -10 Stokes Mortars open hurricane bombardment and vicinity of @ becomes crater. Immediately following this, No. Section (4 guns) under Lieuts F.K. McAlpin and F.H. Hardy push over the HAWTHORNE REDOUBT there establish their guns. 2 guns engage German trenches running N. 2 guns engage those going "S". These guns should be in position at 0.0.

When the 4 Royal Fus. pass through them they will immediately come under the orders of the O.C. that unit.

Should these guns become neutralised the Gun Commander will report to the O.C. Brigade Machine Gun Co. who will give instructions for their further employment.

"Z" day
(continued)

2 Guns of No 2 Section under 2/Lieut. J.O. LATER will be attached to 2/Lancashire Fusiliers and under the orders of the Off. Comdg that Unit.

2 Guns of No 3 Section under 2/Lieut G.M. CREASEY will advance at 0.0 on the left of the LANCS FUSRS push round them and establish themselves at (52) getting a Vertical searching fire on (12) - (21) with one gun and on (26) with the other and continue fire till 1.20. observer must be put out to watch advancing troops and fire effect. at 1.25 move guns forward to (41) establish and range on (75) and R.6.Q.6.d.q.o and wire beyond.

2 Guns under Lieut P.A. BYRNE will advance on the Right of the 2/Royal Scots reaching a point Q.11.a.4.0 one gun engaging BEAUMONT ALLEY and one (41) & (98) these guns will be re-inforced at 0.20 by

2 Guns under 2/Lieut. O.J.P. DUFFY.

At 1.00 traversing fire will be kept up between (41) - (51) lifting fire at 1.15.

At 1.25 all 4 guns move forward as rapidly as possible to (98) establishing and covering our troops who will be wire cutting from R.7.A.6.2. to R.1.c.16.50.

At 0.20 the guns from the BOWERY, ESSEX ST, and PILK St. with O.C. Company will advance across the German trenches through & Cemetary Q.11.d.27. to Right of 2nd Objective.

4.
FIRE
DIV: OPER. ORDER 36 para 11 and 24.
Bde OPER. ORDER 55 para 24.
" " " appendix "J" N.º1. d. (Gas)
" " " N.º 56 para 3 Reconnaissance.

5.
SAFETY
Gun will cease overhead fire as soon as our assaulting troops are seen...

| | |
|---|---|
| Safety (continued) | 2 degrees of safety (tangent sights raised 400 yards) will be used.<br>All guns must be prepared to cover our flanks in case of counter attack. |
| Rate of Fire | During hours that guns are firing, every gun will fire at least 1 belt every 20 minutes. |
| 7. Headquarters<br>Machine Gun. | 86th Brigade junction of Essex St & Broadway<br>" " " PIR St & Cardiff Trench |
| 8. Communication | Telephone between :-<br>Machine Gun Hqrs.<br>Brigade Headqrs.<br>Bowery<br>Newtownards.<br>Runners will be with M.G Headquarters. All officers servants will act as runners to their officers.<br>After M.G Headqrs have moved forward, signallers will collect up instruments and move forward and establish communication from the German 2nd line. |
| Ammunition Supply S.A.A. | Each gun going forward will carry a short length belt (25 rounds) in his belt or any handy position.<br>Team short belts ............... 175<br>N.C.O one box ............... 250<br>No 1 and 2 - each ............... 500<br>No 3,4 & 5 two boxes each ............... 1500<br>Total going over with gun - 2425<br>Ammunition dumps are established at :-<br>King St., PIR St., ...<br>The company reserve of 4500 |

**S.A.A.** (2.000) will be divided on 4 limbers ready to move forward when required.

Officer in charge of teams will personally assure themselves that their ammunition carriers are thoroughly acquainted with these Dumps and also their duties.

There are also spare belts packed 2 in a sandbag at these Dumps, the bags are marked with a black circle O on both sides of bags.

**PISTOL.** Pistol ammunition can be obtained from the C.S.M.

**BOMBS.** 2 bombs per man will be carried by those Nos. who do not carry rifles.

**WATER** A plentiful supply of water must be maintained at each gun till "Z" day. Then Commanders of guns must see their carriers bring up water.

Teams must be cautioned about drawing water from wells etc. in the German lines, till it has been tested to see if it is fit for drinking and cooking.

**RATIONS** Rations will be issued as usual until "Z" day. On "Z" day rations for the troops will be drawn direct from re-filling point in the cooks carts and will move forward under instructions received from Brigade.

If circumstances permit, the ration train will proceed to MAILLY WOOD on "Z" day. The re-filling point for the following day will be on the MAILLY-HÉDAUVILLE road alongside MAILLY WOOD close to troops on west side of the road.

**DISTINGUISHING MARKS** Will consist of a number of patches

**DISTINGUISHING MARKS (continued)**

Stretcher bearers, will wear a triangular piece of tin on the outside of their haversacks.

Runners Badge - Blue armlet with white line
Carriers letter "C" in white sewn on sleeve.

The Divisional patch will also be worn on both sleeves.

Crossed Vickers Guns & Crown painted red on front of steel helmets.

**EQUIPMENT**

"Fighting Order" reversed on back
Nos. 1, 2, 3 & 6 without rifles
            " " shorts.
No. 1. carries 1st belt case.
No. 2. spare haversack with spare parts

The following will also be carried by all ranks:-
            Rations for Day
            Emergency Rations
            Field Dressing
            Identity Disc
            Gas Helmets
            2 Sandbags
            W.P. Sheet
            Clasp Knife

Officers must also carry Revolver, Field Glasses, Note Books & Map, either 1/10,000 or 1/20,000 Beaumont Trench Map, Sheet 57d S.E. or Sheet 57 S.E.
N.C.O's must also carry Note Books.

**WATCHES**

Watches will be synchronised daily, an Officer being detailed to go to Headquarters each day to obtain correct time.

**GAS**

Officer in charge at the Brewery, ESSEX STREET, and KENT WYNARDS will take steps

**GAS**
(continued).

to see that their Gas Sprayers are in good working order, and that additional Jars of Solution are available. The Company Gas N.C.O. has been sent round these Sprayers, but Officers are responsible they are ready for use.

Great care must be taken of the Box respirators, and attention is called to Circular re "Alternative Method of Wearing Anti-Gas helmets during Gas Alert."

**16.**
**Kits, Stores and Orderly Room documents**

All officers will carry with them what they require, Gun numbers are not to carry anything but their own Kit and the material required for the work allotted to them.

All Officers Kits will be securely rolled up in their Kit bags or Valises plainly marked with owners name etc., inside and out.

These will be stored at the Company Dump at ACHEUX.

All Company stores will be packed in boxes or sacks and placed in Company Dump under charge of C.Q.M.S. and L/Cpl Morris.

Mens Overcoats rolled in bundles of 5 together with their packs will be stored in the cellar No 3 Billet in MAILLY MAILLET.

**17.**
**MEDICAL**

All troops are reminded that the care of the wounded is the duty of Regimental Stretcher bearers and Field Ambulances. Fighting troops are forbidden to accompany wounded men to the Dressing Stations.

**18.**
**LOOTING**

Looting is a Court Martial Crime, punishable by "Death".

| | |
|---|---|
| 19 GUNS in DANGER of CAPTURE | Gun Commanders must instruct their men how to destroy a Machine Gun unless, in the event of a gun being in danger of being captured. |
| 20 IMPORTANCE OF THE ATTACK | It is of the utmost importance for this attack to be successful and all Officers N.C.O's and men must exert their maximum effort to make the attack a success and upon the energy and cheerfulness of the Officers largely depends the success of the engagement. |
| 21 TROOPS HOLDING FRONT LINE | During the bombardment the Brigade front will be held by 2 Companies of Royal Fusiliers and 2 Companies of Lancashire Fusiliers. |
| 22 ROUTE | On Y/Z night the Company will move from ACHEUX by the following route:<br>ROTTEN ROW<br>NEW TRACK<br>BROADWAY<br>2nd AVENUE<br>Point P.8. d.80.45. where ROTTEN ROW leaves ACHEUX WOOD by 21.4 above mentioned point to be cleared by 21.40 |
| 23 PROGRAMME of INFANTRY ADVANCE | See Brigade Operation Orders Appendix B (issued copy) |
| 24 PRISONERS | Any Prisoners taken will be escorted back to our original front line and handed over to O.C. to be imprisoned. |
| 25 TRANSPORT | The Transport Sergeant will have the Ammunition limbers, Cooks cart and water cart ready to move down and bring up from Brigade |

Trench
traffic

On "Z" day communication trenches will be reserved as follows:—
UP traffic. Withington, Tipperary and 2nd Avenue.
DOWN   "   Gabion Avenue, Broadway

E.K.E.[?] Woth Captain,
Commanding 86th Bde
Machine Gun Coy.

Copy No 1 & 2  Office
         3.   War Diary
         4.   86th Brigade
         5.  Lt McAlpin K.J.
         6.   " Hardy H.J.
         7.   " Stevenson J.B.J.
         8. 2/Lt Later J.O.
         9.   " Creasey G.M.
        10.   " Duffy D.J.P.
        11.  Lt Milne W.
        12.   " Byrne P.A.
        13a C.S.M. Digby W.
        13  87th M.G. Co

In the Field.
June 22nd 1916.
        14  88th M.G. Co

Operation Order N° 16
Major E Beckwith M.C. Comg 86th Company
Machine Gun Corps.

23rd October 1916

Reference Map.
57C. S.W. 1/20,000 9
Trench Diagram N° 3 of Oct. 20th 1/10,000.

**General information** 1. The XV Corps will continue the attack on October _____ at an hour ZERO which will be notified later. The 8th Australian Brigade, 5th Div.n will be on the left of the 86th Brigade, and the 87th Bde on the right.

**Objective** 2. The Brigade will assault to BAYONET TRENCH and consolidate it. Us BACON TRENCH and from there, move forward and dig in as close as possible to BARLEY TRENCH.

**PLAN of ATTACK** 3. Battalions will attack with four companies in line of Company column i.e. In four waves. During the night of the 24th Battalions will be formed up in the forward lines and shell holes well closed up in the above order. The German trenches will be subjected to a slow preliminary bombardment until ZERO. There will be no intense bombardment before that hour. Artillery programme later.

At ZERO hour a heavy artillery barrage will open over a zone of about 150 yards on either side of BAYONET TRENCH.

Immediately this barrage opens the attack will move forward upon BAYONET TRENCH. Having captured BAYONET TRENCH there will be a pause of 20 minutes

Operation Orders
By
Major. A. Morris Commanding
88th Machine Gun Company
24th October 1916

**I Operations** — No 1. 2 & 3 Sections will move into position in Gurd Trench tomorrow, these positions have already been reconitered.

**II Positions** — Guns will be in position by 3 pm and fire observation obtained.

**III Water** — 30 Tins of Water will be sent up to Delville Valley by pack transport tomorrow from where it will be drawn by Sections.

**IV Rations** — One days rations will be carried by each man also the unconsumed portion of the days rations.

**V Dress** — Gloves and leather Jerkins will be worn whilst in the Trenches.

**VI Iron Rations & Field dressings** — Iron Rations and field dressings will be carried by all ranks, the Iron Rations are not to be consumed unless by permission of an Officer.

**VII Reserve Ammunition** — 10 Belt Boxes will be taken for each Gun. Reserve ammunition will be obtained (left Sector) from O.C. 86th Machine Gun Company, (Right Sector) from deep dugout in Gurd Trench.

**VIII Zero** — Zero will be obtained from the nearest Infantry Commander, in case of Communication failing.

**IX Transport** — 39 Pack Animals will be at Company Headquarters at 11.15 am on the 25th inst.

**X Communication** — Two men per Section will be detailed to act as Despatch Carriers.

**XI C.HQ.** — The position of Company Head quarters will be as Heretofore.

Major Commanding
88th Machine Gun Company

29th Division.
86th Infantry Brigade.
------

86th BRIGADE.

MACHINE GUN COMPANY

NOVEMBER 1 9 1 6

Vol. X

War Diary.
of the
86th Company Machine Gun Corps.

Volume
IX

From 1st November 1916
to
30th November 1916

NO. IX

Army Form C. 2118.

# WAR DIARY
## or
## INTELLIGENCE SUMMARY.
*(Erase heading not required.)*

Instructions regarding War Diaries and Intelligence Summaries are contained in F. S. Regs., Part II. and the Staff Manual respectively. Title pages will be prepared in manuscript.

| Place | Date | Hour | Summary of Events and Information | Remarks and references to Appendices |
|---|---|---|---|---|
| | 1916 | | | |
| CORBIE | 12 to 17 | 10.00hrs | The Company were in Rest from 12 to 16th Nov. during which time the Company was reclothed. Equipment made good & Gas Equipment tested. | |
| | | 15th Nov | Gun Instruction carried out. Arms & Physical drill exercised. A draft of men arrived from Base 2nd inst. O. Condy Company (Major S. Beckwith) proceeded on leave to the United Kingdom 2nd inst. | |
| | 18th Nov 18th Nov | 10.01 9.44.00 | The Company moved by road Route to BILLETS at Meaulte, The Company moved by Mary route to Bivouacs at CARNOY Company relieves 102/6yth M.G.C. in the line. 2 guns in the front line, 2 in the 2nd line, 4 in 3rd line & 5 in Reserve at GUILLE-MONT | |
| | | | 4th Nov CAPT. P.A. BYRNE left to # CAMIER for Course of Instruction in TACTICS relinquishing 2ft/Knot. 2nd Lt. de Eurkertel fd. United Kingdom to Join G. Reens Company at GRANTHAM. Lieut: Robinson proceeded to CAMIER 24th for Course of Instruction. | |

Army Form C. 2118.

# WAR DIARY
## or
## INTELLIGENCE SUMMARY.
*(Erase heading not required.)*

| Place | Date | Hour | Summary of Events and Information | Remarks and references to Appendices |
|---|---|---|---|---|
| | 1916 | | | |
| COILLEMONT | 29/3/16 | | O.C.Coy. (Major E.Beckwith) returned from United Kingdom. Lieut A.D. RIX posted to Company from Base. Lieut E.B. FLETCHER admitted to hospital. No casualties during the Month. | |
| | 31/3/16 | | | |

E.Beckwith Major
Comdg. 86 G. Machine Gun Corps.

End Mar. 1916

29th Division.

86th Infantry Brigade.

------

86th BRIGADE

MACHINE GUN COMPANY

DECEMBER 1 9 1 6

# Confidential

### War Diary
of
### 86th Company, Machine Gun Corps

From December 1st to December 31st 1916.

Volume 10.

Army Form C. 2118.

# WAR DIARY
## or
## INTELLIGENCE SUMMARY

VOL X

(Erase heading not required.)

Instructions regarding War Diaries and Intelligence Summaries are contained in F. S. Regs., Part II. and the Staff Manual respectively. Title Pages will be prepared in manuscript.

| Place | Date | Hour | Summary of Events and Information | Remarks and references to Appendices |
|---|---|---|---|---|
| Guillemont | 1st December 1916 | | Hostile activity below normal, LES BŒUFS and MORVAL shrug chiefly shelled. Weather continues frosty and misty. | |
| | 2nd December | | Enemy Artillery somewhat below normal. Our Artillery fairly active during the morning. We established a Machine Gun at the S. End of CIGEL TRENCH lately taken over from the 125 Infty (French). Weather: Frosty, slight snow in showers at Midday. Enemy Artillery quiet. | |
| | 3rd Dect. | | Prisoner brought in states that the Strength of Troops in Front/ is about to be from 60 to 100 days, not less. Heavy shelling and the removal at day all Ross Machine Guns of the 3rd Company are in the front line (British). | |
| | | | MOON TRENCH) Our Rifles grenadiers are in the Support line (probably TRENCH) the guns fire sub rose Prospect, the surface of which is narrow and are protected from view by Tarpaulins, or other Head cover which they are usually in position day and night. | |
| | | | Weather: Foggy. Enemy Opened a heavy bombardment on our front & support line at about 11 o'clock | |
| | 4th Dect. | | | |

Army Form C. 2118.

# WAR DIARY
## or
## INTELLIGENCE SUMMARY.
*(Erase heading not required.)*

Instructions regarding War Diaries and Intelligence Vol X
Summaries are contained in F. S. Regs., Part II.
and the Staff Manual respectively. Title pages
will be prepared in manuscript.

| Place | Date | Hour | Summary of Events and Information | Remarks and references to Appendices |
|---|---|---|---|---|
| | 1916 | | Continued :- | |
| GUILLEMONT | 4th Dec. | | Two of our Machine Guns were put out of action and the teams buried. Stretcher bearers to the Company sent for. | |
| | | | Otherwise the day was quiet. | |
| | | | Weather Dull, misty and drizzly. | |
| | 5th Dec. | | Company commenced two new rifle and deep dugouts for two guns and teams in STRAIGHT TRENCH in the Reserve Line. New Gun positions were sited at FLANK AVENUE and 150 x E 8 MORVAL in the Strong Points. | |
| | | | Weather - Milder. Mid-day Sunny. | |
| | 6th Dec. | | No event of importance occurred during the period. The reliefs were carried out without event. | |
| | 9th Dec. | | | |
| to | | | The Company was relieved in the line by the 59th Machine Gun Company. | |
| 10th Dec. | | | On completion of relief, the company moved by march route to MEAULTE. | |
| MEAULTE | | | Weather: Heavy rain & Cold. | |

Army Form C. 2118.

# WAR DIARY
## or
## INTELLIGENCE SUMMARY.
(Erase heading not required.)

Instructions regarding War Diaries and Intelligence Summaries are contained in F. S. Regs., Part II. and the Staff Manual respectively. Title pages will be prepared in manuscript.

| Place | Date | Hour | Summary of Events and Information | Remarks and references to Appendices |
|---|---|---|---|---|
| | 1916 | | | |
| MEAULTE | 11th Oct | | The Company rested in billets. Preparatory to moving to SAISSEMONT. Weather, Rain. | |
| | 12th Oct. | | The Transport proceeded by road to SAISSEMONT billetting one night at DAOURS. | |
| | | | Company remained in Billets at MEAULTE. Weather, Cold & Showery. | |
| | 13th Oct | | Company Entrained at EDGEHILL, DERNACOURT, for LONGPRÉ arrived 9 pm and marched to SAISSEMONT (4 miles). Weather Dull & Slight rain. | |
| | 14th Oct to 17th Oct | | The Company were re-issued with underwear & Clothing. Gun equipment overhauled & cleaned. Billets improved. | |
| | 18th Oct. | | Company marched from SAISSEMONT to Billets at AILLY SUR SOMME (6 miles) by Lieut J.V.B. Simmonds. | |
| | | | No.1 Section. | |
| | 19th Oct. | | Sergt. Roran Promoted Company Quartermaster Sergent and posted to S&Co | |

Army Form C. 2118.

# WAR DIARY
## or
## INTELLIGENCE SUMMARY.

(Erase heading not required.)

Instructions regarding War Diaries and Intelligence Summaries are contained in F. S. Regs., Part II. and the Staff Manual respectively. Title pages will be prepared in manuscript.

| Place | Date | Hour | Summary of Events and Information | Remarks and references to Appendices |
|---|---|---|---|---|
| ALLY- SUR- SOMME | 1916 20th Decr. to 30th Decr. | | The Company carried out Instructional work Drill & Route marches. Christmas was kept up by the Company. Accommodation being found in the Local School. A dinner & concert was provided & much enjoyed by the Company. No dinner being celebrated at Welles. Lieutenant G.L. Dimond who joined the Company 18th Decr. was accidentally killed on the 29th Decr. by a Tram. | |

30th December
1916

Edward Dreyfus Major
Comdg 86 Coy. Machine Gun Corps.

Vol 12

## Confidential
### War Diary
### of
## 86th Company, Machine Gun Corps.

From 1st January 1917 to 31st January 1917

(Volume XI).

Army Form C. 2118.

# WAR DIARY
## or
## INTELLIGENCE SUMMARY.
(Erase heading not required.)

Vol XI

| Place | Date | Hour | Summary of Events and Information | Remarks and references to Appendices |
|---|---|---|---|---|
| | 1917 | | | |
| AILLY-SUR- SOMME | 1st January | | The Company remained in Rest Billets. Drill classes and Lewis Gun Instruction were carried out. Interfortball games were played with other units in the Brigade. a Lewis Gun & Musketry were available all ranks having with Rifle Practice. | |
| | 9th January | | On the 2nd January a field day under the Brigadier was carried out. The following promotions & appointments were made in the Company. | |
| | | | N. 20973 a/Sgt. W. McNab promoted to Sergeant vice Ronan to UK. 23.12.16 | |
| | | | 13635 a/Sgt. L. Orris " " " vice Duffy reduced 23.12.16 | |
| | | | 9665 a/Sgt. Morris " " " to complete Est. 19.11.16 | |
| | | | 20995 a/L/Sgt. Morris — L/Sgt appt a/Sergeant 23.12.16 | |
| | | | 20934 Corb George appointed a/Sergeant vice McNab. 23.12.16 | |
| | | | 30946 a/Cpl Murphy promoted Corporal and appt a/Sgt 23.12.16 | |
| | | | 4527?.. a/Cpl Starr promoted to Cpl. 23.12.16. 20982 a/Cpl Edward promoted Cpl 23.12.16 | |
| | | | 26807 a/Cpl Fawn — 11.10.16. 20910 L/Cpl Morris appd a/Cpl 23.12.16 | |
| | | | 2613 L/Cpl Hughes — a/Cpl 23.12.16. +2061 Cpl Ind 5 vice Cpl Duffy | |
| | 10th January | | The Company proceeded by March Route to CROUY & Billets | |

Army Form C. 2118.

# WAR DIARY
## or
## INTELLIGENCE SUMMARY.
(Erase heading not required.)

Instructions regarding War Diaries and Intelligence Summaries are contained in F. S. Regs., Part II. and the Staff Manual respectively. Title pages will be prepared in manuscript.

| Place | Date | Hour | Summary of Events and Information | Remarks and references to Appendices |
|---|---|---|---|---|
| | 1917 | | | |
| CROUY | 11th January | | The Company remained one night and moved to HANGEST Railway Station and there entrained for CORBIE arriving at this town at about mid-day. The Davenport Moret by March Route to CORBIE arriving about 4 p.m. | |
| CORBIE to TREUX | 13th January | | Company marched from CORBIE to TREUX. | |
| | 15th January | | Company marched from TREUX to GUILLEMONT and relieved the 50th M.G. Company in the MORVAL SECTOR with 2 guns. | |
| GUILLEMONT | 17th January | | Lieutenants Robinson & J.H.ORPEN to be Temporary Lieutenants. Enemy activity much below normal. | |
| | 23rd Jany | | The Company was relieved in the line by 88th M.G. Company the Company returning to Camp at MANSELL The following promotions were made in the Company. 19020925 A/Sgt T. Morris. T. Granted Temporary Lance Corporal I. appointed L/Cpl. Sergt Murphy. E. appointed Sergt. 10910 A/Cpl Morris. W. promoted Corporal. | |
| MANSELL | 25th January | | 12 Guns under Lieuts J.H.ORPEN. K.M.MOIR. C.D. RIX. went into line to assist in an operation to be carried out by the 87th Brigade | |

Army Form C. 2118.

# WAR DIARY
## or
## INTELLIGENCE SUMMARY.
(Erase heading not required.)

Instructions regarding War Diaries and Intelligence Summaries are contained in F. S. Regs., Part II. and the Staff Manual respectively. Title pages will be prepared in manuscript.

| Place | Date | Hour | Summary of Events and Information | Remarks and references to Appendices |
|---|---|---|---|---|
| | 1917 | | | |
| MORVAL | 26th January | | Throughout the day all guns were registered on the areas allotted to them. Temporary emplacements were made and flash blinding screens erected. Shell explosions intensely cold. | |
| | 27th Jany | | Zero was timed for 05.30 by this time all preparations were complete. The artillery curtain fell and all the Machine Guns of the Division opened fire on their areas. Incidences with attached heaps and overs, the attacking troops were successful and gained their objective. Approximately 380 to 750 prisoners were taken. Our casualties being very slight. One of the Machine Gun Company our casualties were 7 O. Ranks wounded and two guns knocked out. Throughout the following nights to 31st Jany all guns searched throughout the enemy lines of communication trenches. | messages attached |
| | 31st Jany | | A relief was carried out with 88th M.G.C. which was completed without incident. | |

# WAR DIARY
## or
## INTELLIGENCE SUMMARY.

Army Form C. 2118.

| Place | Date | Hour | Summary of Events and Information | Remarks and references to Appendices |
|---|---|---|---|---|
| GUILLEMONT | 31st Jany 1917 | | The strength of the Company is:— 10 Offrs 169 o.Ranks | |
| | | | The work shall continue very dts and frosty | |
| | | | A Park Harrington Comdg 86 Co. Machine Gun Corps | |

## Machine Gun Instructions.

1/ In continuation of 20th Division Order No 83 para. 8. Brigades will station Machine Guns as follows:- (vide map X attached.)

(a) 86th Machine Gun Company — 12 guns in "A" area near the following points:-

          Zones of Fire

4 guns T.12.a.9.9 MOON TRENCH. O.31.c.4.4 — N.36.d.9.6
4 guns U.1.c.3.4. MOON TRENCH. N.36.d.9.6 — N.36.b.4.8.
4 guns U.1.c.5.9.enfilade MOON TRENCH — no fire left of
          N 36. d. 6.1.

(b) 87th Machine Gun Company, — 12 guns in 'B' area near the following points:-
4 guns T.5.a. 8.9 — N.36.c.6.8 — N 35. d. 8. 9.
4 guns ANTELOPE TRENCH
 T.5.c.9.9. Cover valley 200 yds N.E. of FALL TRENCH
4 guns (mobile) N.36.c.5.2. Cover front of attack.

(c) The 88th Machine Gun Company, — 8 guns in 'C' area near the following points:-
2 guns T.6.b.5.7. O.31.c.4.4 — N.36.d.7.0.
2 guns T.6.a.9.7 Defensive purposes covering present
  front lines
4 guns (mobile)
  N.36.d.4.2. Cover right flank of attack.

2/ Rate of Fire:-

2/ (contd.)

From. 0.0 to 0.25 All guns will open barrage fire on targets as detailed in para. 1.

From 0.25 to 0.45 All guns will open bursts of fire on their targets.

At 0.45. Guns will cease fire but hold themselves in readiness to open in the event of a hostile counter-attack, or as targets present themselves; with the exception of the 4 guns at U.1.c.5.9. and T.5.a.8.9. who will continue to fire bursts till 8.0.

3/ <u>Registration</u>
will be carried out at intervals on the days preceeding the attack, care being taken to avoid arousing the suspicion of the enemy.

4/ All the above guns will come under the command of the G.O.C. 87th Brigade from midnight on 26th-29th January 1917. He will be responsible for communicating to them the zero hour.

The above moves will take place under mutual arrangements to be made between Machine Gun Company Commanders concerned.

3

5. <u>Defensive Guns</u>:- The remaining guns of the 87th and 88th Machine Gun Companies not detailed above will be employed for defence under orders to be issued by G.Os C. Left and Right Brigade Groups respectively.

6. <u>Non-Freezing Mixture</u>:- 1/8th of glycerine will be used in the barrel casing of all guns.

7. <u>Ammunition</u>:- 16 boxes of ammunition per gun will be placed with each gun. Reserve dumps will be established in the forward area. All ranks must know the exact position of these dumps.

8. <u>Range-Cards</u>:- Previous to the operation range-cards will be made on the assumption that the position has been taken. The general direction of hostile counter-attack being assumed as coming from MOOR TRENCH.

9. <u>Mobile Section</u>:- The 89th & 88th Companies will both supply one mobile section on the left & right flanks respectively. The object of this section will be to neutralise the enemy's fire & prevent him establishing superiority

either by rifle or machine gun fire.

These sections will follow immediately in the wake of the assaulting wave & reach the captured position as soon as possible after the assaulting troops.

On reaching the captured position the particular duty of these guns will be to meet a hostile counter attack.

---

Detail of Offensive to guns @ paragraph 1. @

No 3. Section T. 12. a. 9. 9. Lieut K. M. Moir

No 4 Section D. 1. c. 3. d 2/Lieut A.B Rix

No 1 Section D. 1. c 5. 9 Lieut A. Mason

Officers will be responsible that their guns are fully equipped before leaving Headquarters.

A limber will be allotted to each Officer taking:-

| | |
|---|---|
| Gun Oil | Range cards |
| Flannelette | Water bottles filled |
| Glycerine | Field glasses |
| Water | Prismatic compasses |
| Spares | Whale Oil |
| 16 Belts brass | 2 days' rations |

Orderlies:- One runner will be attached to each Officer. The servant will also act as orderly.

RUM ISSUE:- Each Officer will take 2 bottles of rum for 2 days. He will issue this rum at his discretion.

Attention is to be paid to paragraphs on Registering + Range cards.

(Sd) E Beckwith Major MC
Commanding 86th Company, M.Gun Corps

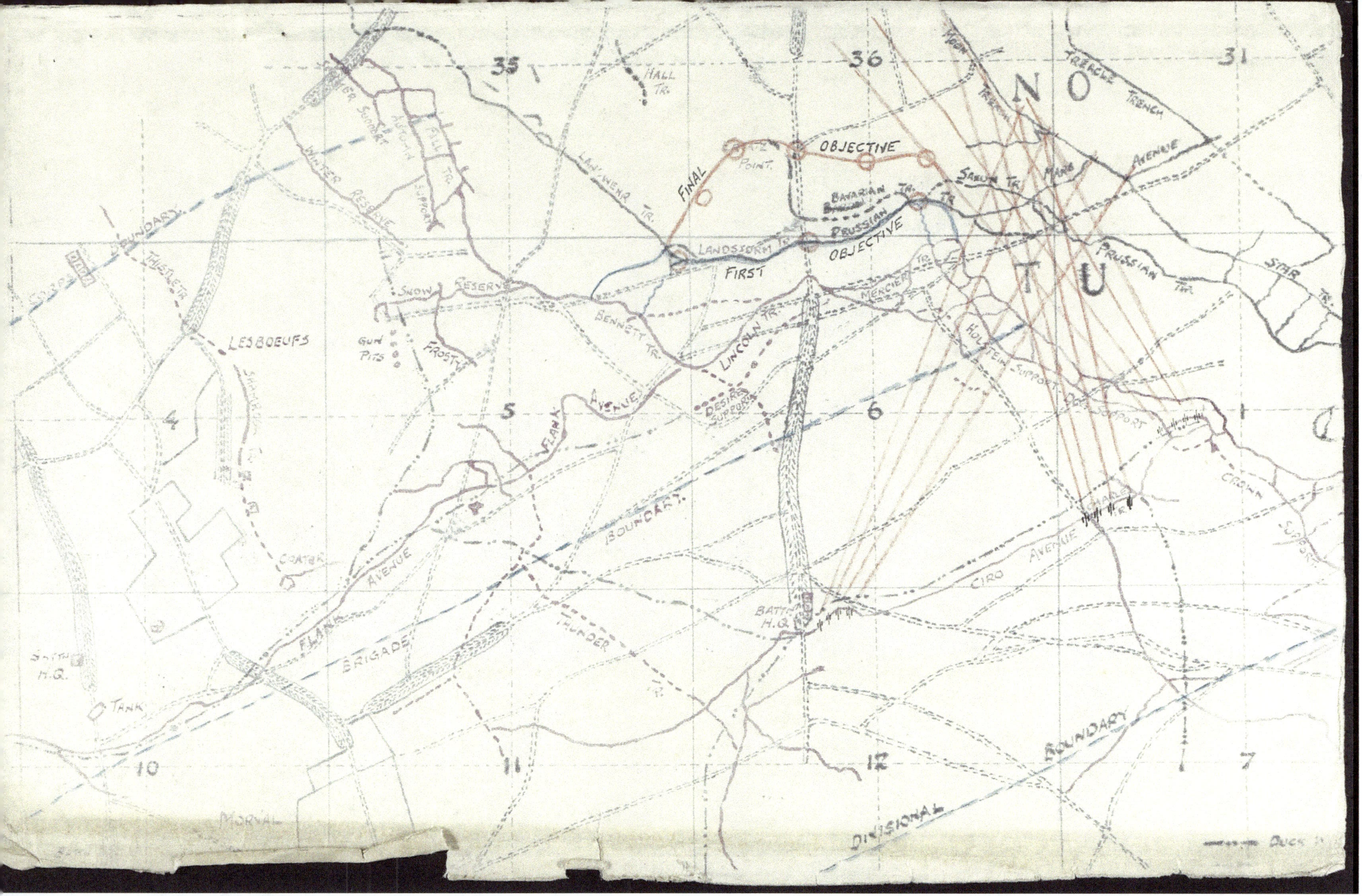

35
HALL TR.
36
N O
TRENCH
TREACLE TRENCH
31
OBJECTIVE
POINT
FINAL
LANDWEHR TR.
WINTER RESERVE
SUPPORT
FALL TR.
BAVARIAN TR.
SABLON TR.
AVENUE
PRUSSIAN
LANDSSORM TR.
FIRST
OBJECTIVE
T U
PRUSSIAN TR.
STAR TR.
BOUNDARY
THISTLE TR.
SNOW
RESERVE
BENNETT TR.
MERCIER TR.
LESBOEUFS
GUN PITS
FROSTY
LINCOLN TR.
HOLSTEIN SUPPORT
4
5
AVENUE
FLANK
DESIRE SUPPORT
6
SUPPORT
CROWN
BOUNDARY
CRATER
AVENUE
CIRO
AVENUE
BATTN H.Q.
FLANK
BRIGADE
THUNDER
TR.
H.Q.
TANK
10
11
12
BOUNDARY
7
MORVAL
DIVISIONAL

Vol 13

Confidential
War Diary
of
86th Company. Machine Gun Corps.
From 1st February 1917 to 28th February 1917.

Volume XII.

# WAR DIARY
## or
## INTELLIGENCE SUMMARY.

VOLUME XII (Erase heading not required.)

Army Form C. 2118.

Instructions regarding War Diaries and Intelligence Summaries are contained in F. S. Regs., Part II. and the Staff Manual respectively. Title pages will be prepared in manuscript.

| Place | Date | Hour | Summary of Events and Information | Remarks and references to Appendices |
|---|---|---|---|---|
| | 1917 | | | |
| GUILLEMONT | 1st Feby | | The part of German line taken by us on the 27th has not be retaken by the Germans although he made several attempts but was beaten off by artillery & machine gun fire. We have had casualties and extended our line slightly to our Right. | |
| | 2nd Feby | | The weather continues extremely cold today, and the continual laugh of time in the trenches is beginning to tell upon the garrisons. One of our machine guns was knocked out and two of the team wounded, this occurred at about 5pm during a Bombardment by our own Artillery on BOSNIA TRENCH. So it is difficult to decide if it was by a short shell of our own or by enemy retaliation. Considerable aircraft activity took place during the day. | |
| | 3rd Feby | | Divisional Routine Orders contained the following message:— Following received from C. in C. Congratulate 29th Division warmly and in particular 1st Border Regiment & 1st Royal Innskilling Fusiliers on the success of their operations carried out 27th January January 17. In forwarding this message the Army Commander wishes to add his congratulations to the C in C's. Success in 10 Corps. Ivor Maxse. | |

Army Form C. 2118.

# WAR DIARY
or
## INTELLIGENCE SUMMARY.
(Erase heading not required.)

Instructions regarding War Diaries and Intelligence Summaries are contained in F. S. Regs., Part II. and the Staff Manual respectively. Title pages will be prepared in manuscript.

| Place | Date | Hour | Summary of Events and Information | Remarks and references to Appendices |
|---|---|---|---|---|
| | 1917 | | | |
| GUILLEMONT | 4th February | | Officer Commanding 60th Machine Gun Company went round Support Sector of Gun positions, preparatory to taking over on the 7th inst. Enemy Aeroplanes very active over our lines. | |
| | 7th February | | Considerable activity by our Artillery during the early night. The Company was relieved in the line by the 60th C.M.G.C. relief commenced at about 11pm and was complete by 10.30pm. The relief passed off without incident. The Company then went into camp at MANSELL. | |
| BUSSY by DAOURS | 8th February | | The Company moved to BUSSY being conveyed by omnibus. The transport moving by Road. The Men were billeted here. | |
| | 9th February | | General cleaning up of the Company and Guns | |
| | 10th February | | Company drill and overhauling of Equipment and Ammunition. | |
| | 11th February | | Church parade. A party of 1/10 gunners from this Base depot joined for duty with the Company. | |
| | 12th February | | The Company was inspected by the acting Brigadier General (about Colonel BECKWITH). The severe frost still continues. | |

Army Form C. 2118.

# WAR DIARY
## or
## INTELLIGENCE SUMMARY.
(Erase heading not required.)

| Place | Date | Hour | Summary of Events and Information | Remarks and references to Appendices |
|---|---|---|---|---|
| | 1917 February | | | |
| BUSSY-LES-DAOURS | 13th | | Company Parade. Marching order. Inspection of kit and arms. Lectures on promotion of rest. Care and wear of Lewis Gun. Discharge & football. | |
| | 14th February | | Afternoon Gun instruction and Company Drill carried out. | |
| | 19th February | | Gun instruction and Company Drill carried out. A practical scheme was set in during the daylight hours by night. An attack practice by the Brigade was carried out in the vicinity. The scheme was set in very rapidly. Road & Railways into a hot star sign. The troops have to be taken were happily put. | |
| | 19th February 20th February | | Full use of transport moved by Road to MANSEL CAMP. The Company moved by march route to CORBIE from thence to MANSELL CAMP by Train where the Company went for the night. | |
| HAIEWOOD | 21st February | | COPSE SECTOR of the firing line. The Company relieved the 50th Machine Gun Company in the NORTH. 14 Guns were mounted, Two being in Reserve at HAIEWOOD. Mounted 60 A.A. Guns. The weather has been quite fair. | |

# WAR DIARY or INTELLIGENCE SUMMARY

Army Form C. 2118.

| Place | Date | Hour | Summary of Events and Information | Remarks and references to Appendices |
|---|---|---|---|---|
| HAREWOOD | 22nd July | | Enemy Artillery active, shelling the rear Dug-outs that have been recently held. Our Artillery retaliating freely. Afternoon enemy aeroplane flying high came over but was driven off by A.A. guns. | |
| | 24th July | | Warning order received notifying the Company that an operation would probably take place on or about 27th July. Lieut. Kenny reported sick from the line, suffering from shell shock and was evacuated. His place in the line being taken by Lieut. Stainton. The company has now been formed 1 year. | |
| | 27th July | | A patrol of the S.W. Borderers moved out in mid day patrolled and occupied POTSDAM TRENCH meeting with little or no opposition from the enemy. Major Beckwith, Lieut Fegris-Hope and 1 Gun & team occupied a Gun position in the above German Trench. Remaining there until ordered to withdraw to our own line at 5 am 27th by the O.C. Border. | |

2449 Wt. W14957/M90 750,000 1/16 J.B.C. & A. Forms/C.2118/12.

**Army Form C. 2118.**

# WAR DIARY
## or
## INTELLIGENCE SUMMARY

*(Erase heading not required.)*

Instructions regarding War Diaries and Intelligence Summaries are contained in F. S. Regs., Part II. and the Staff Manual respectively. Title Pages will be prepared in manuscript.

| Place | Date | Hour | Summary of Events and Information | Remarks and references to Appendices |
|---|---|---|---|---|
| SAILLY SAILLISEL | 27th Feby | 1917 | Final arrangements made to carry out an attack on the front line trench from U.H.6.65.15 to U.8.a.25.95. Operation to take place at 5.25am (ZERO) 28th Feby 17. Enemy Artillery very active, dropping shrapnel on the HAIE WOOD ROAD and LOUSEWOOD. German Aeroplanes also active and flying low, one being driven down by Machine Gun & A.A. Gun fire. Troops taking part in the operation moved up during the night to their allotted areas. All Machine Guns got into their Battle emplacements. | |
|  | 28th Feby | 5.25 am | At 5.25am the time laid down for the Barrage to fall all troops were in position. The Barrage at its allotted hour, the assault made & the position carried. (Orders, maps & reports will be attached to March War Diary). | |

Edward Shuttleworth Major.
Cmdg 8th C. Machine Gun Coy.
28th Feby 1917

Vol. 13

Confidential

War Diary

of

86th Company, Machine Gun Corps.

From 1st March 1917 to 31st March 1917.

Volume XIII.

Army Form C. 2118.

# WAR DIARY
## or
## INTELLIGENCE SUMMARY

(Erase heading not required.)

86th Machine Gun Coypl.

MARCH 1917 VOLUME XIII

| Place | Date 1917 | Hour | Summary of Events and Information | Remarks and references to Appendices |
|---|---|---|---|---|
| HAIE WOOD | 1st March | | The situation in our newly taken trenches remained unchanged. The Enemy Artillery are very busy throughout the day night the day night and small bombing raids were put up, but all resulted in failure on our flank. Our Artillery maintained a steady fire throughout the night. He three machine Guns in P(?+S)DAM TRENCH where re-inforced by 2 others drawn from CHEESE SUPPORT. A short precis of the Machine Gun operations is attached. | |
| | 2nd March | | The day was fairly quiet on both sides. During the afternoon a number of Tear shells were thrown over into the HAIE WOOD VALLEY, and the DUCKBOARDS to the CHATEAU, SAILLY SAILLISEL were knocked about. | |
| | 3rd March | | All accept three machine guns were withdrawn from the line trench. The Company was relieved in the line by the 61st Bo coypl. 4 guns. and the Guards Brigade 7 guns. During the relief a large number... | |

# WAR DIARY
## or
## INTELLIGENCE SUMMARY

*(Erase heading not required.)*

Army Form C. 2118.

| Place | Date 1917 | Hour | Summary of Events and Information | Remarks and references to Appendices |
|---|---|---|---|---|
| HAIE WOOD | 3rd March | | Continued — number of "Tear Shells" were sent over for this time. Some Austrian among the Troops. The relief was completed by 11 p.m. The Company then marched to WEDGE WOOD for the night. No casualties occurred during the relief. | |
| WEDGE WOOD | 4th March | | The Company marched to the PLATEAU and there entrained for BUIRE and from thence moved by march route to Billets at TREUX | |
| TREUX | 5th March | | Good accommodation for the Company exists in this village. The Brigadier General inspected the Transport and Billets. The Company was employed in general cleaning up and unloading of Transport. | |
| | 6th March | | Remainder of deficiencies and filling up vacancies with the recently arrived draft. Inspection of Ammunition &c. | |

Army Form C. 2118.

# WAR DIARY or INTELLIGENCE SUMMARY

(Erase heading not required.)

Instructions regarding War Diaries and Intelligence Summaries are contained in F. S. Regs., Part II. and the Staff Manual respectively. Title Pages will be prepared in manuscript.

| Place | Date 1917 | Hour | Summary of Events and Information | Remarks and references to Appendices |
|---|---|---|---|---|
| TREUX | 7th March | | Drill, marching and Rifle exercises also cleaning of Arms & Ammn. | |
| | 8th March | | was carried out. The following message to the 29th Division was received from General Sir H.S. Rawlinson Bart. K.C.B. K.C.V.O. "Please convey to 29th Division and specially to 86th Brigade my congratulations on their successful attack yesterday. The tenacity in holding on to POTSDAM TRENCH and its efficient support by the artillery were deserving of high praise. The plan of attack was well conceived by the Divisional Commander & Staff and very gallantly executed by the 1st Roy: Dublin Fusiliers and 2nd Royal Fusiliers. From Lieut: General. J.R. The Earl of Cavan K.P.C.B. M.V.O. "Please convey to 86th Brigade my hearty congratulations and thanks for grit and tenacity during a trying day. Capture of POTSDAM TRENCH was quite up to GALLIPOLI form. 4 to 5 | |

Army Form C. 2118.

# WAR DIARY
## or
## INTELLIGENCE SUMMARY

*(Erase heading not required.)*

Instructions regarding War Diaries and Intelligence Summaries are contained in F. S. Regs., Part II. and the Staff Manual respectively. Title Pages will be prepared in manuscript.

| Place | Date | Hour | Summary of Events and Information | Remarks and references to Appendices |
|---|---|---|---|---|
| TREUX | 8th MARCH 1917 | | the utmost importance and I know the 86th will hold on and keep it. Artillery Support and barrage quite admirable. P.T. Arms Drill and Gun Instruction was carried out. Weather. Frosty. | |
| | 9th March | | P.T. and Route march. Inspection of Transport by G.O.C. Weather. Snow. | |
| | 10th March | | Gun Drill & Equipment Inspection. Weather. Very dull & rainy. | |
| | 11th March | | Church parade. Weather. Dull. | |
| | 12th March | | Tactical scheme. Moving into action from Limber & of Annuals. Weather. Dull & cold. | |
| | 13th March | | Tactical scheme. Machine Guns in the Advanced Guard. Weather. Snow Showy. | |

Army Form C. 2118.

# WAR DIARY
or
## INTELLIGENCE SUMMARY
(Erase heading not required.)

| Place | Date | Hour | Summary of Events and Information | Remarks and references to Appendices |
|---|---|---|---|---|
| TREUX | 14th March 1917 | | P.J. Arms and Gun drill | |
| | | | Promotions Etc | |
| | | | 45272. Corp. C. Storm to be a/Lance Sergt. d/22.2.17. vice 28807 a/L.Sgt Dawn to Sgt. | |
| | | | 42462 Pte. Chapman W.E. to be a/cpl. d/ 1.3.17 vice 21013 Hughes wounded. | |
| | | | 20907 Pte. W. Waldron to be a/Corp. d/1.3.17 vice Corp. Allen transferred. | |
| | | | 20957 Pte. W. Murphy to be a/Corp. d/5.3.17 vice 9491 Dawney returned to A/Sgt. | |
| | | | 28807 a/Lance Sergt. Dawn reverts to Corporal on admission to F.A. 31.2.17 | |
| | 15th March | | Weather fine. Studies at Stores. | |
| | | | P.J. Tactical Scheme "The Attack" | |
| | | | Weather Even Rain. | |
| | 16th March | | P.J. Sec. & Pl. Kneeling, Running, Standing, Kneeling & Sand Throwing. | |
| | | | Weather fine. | |

**Army Form C. 2118.**

# WAR DIARY
## or
## INTELLIGENCE SUMMARY
*(Erase heading not required.)*

| Place | Date | Hour | Summary of Events and Information | Remarks and references to Appendices |
|---|---|---|---|---|
| TROUN | 17th March | | P.D. Route in Marching order. Weather from Dry | |
| | 18th March | | Church Parade. Reinforcement of 3 Sergts, Hillman & Servant with 17 men to B??. Gone from Base Depot. 9743.1000 Pte. Redmond T. appointed L/Cpl (unpaid) 17.3.17. Weather. Cloudy & Rain. | |
| | 19th March | | Route march and Packing of kits in preparation to move. Weather. Heavy rain during night - fair during day. | |
| | 20th March | | The Transport moved by road to Allery. The Company entrained at Killshill at 12 noon arriving at ARRAINES about 3 p.m. and then marched to Billets at ALLERY arriving about 6 p.m. Weather. Strong winds accompanied by showers. | |

# WAR DIARY or INTELLIGENCE SUMMARY

Army Form C. 2118.

| Place | Date | Hour | Summary of Events and Information | Remarks and references to Appendices |
|---|---|---|---|---|
| ALLERY | 1917 | | | |
| | 21st March | | G.T., Drill & Rifle Exercises. Worker. Ins & Bry. | |
| | 22nd March | | G.T., Bombthrowing, Rapid Shooting, Stoppages on Range. Classes:- Range taking - Signalling. The Transport arrived after 3 days T.C.R. Weather. Fine. Very cold. | |
| | 23rd March | | C.Q.M.S. Batt joined for duty from 4.5 Company. 9 O. Ranks joined for duty from Base depot. G.T., Drill & Rifle exercises, Gun drill - working over uneven ground. Lecture by Lieut. K.M. Morris "Head of L of Lon and Fire orders. Classes:- Bomb throwing, Revolver shooting, Stoppages, Range finding & Signalling. Weather. Rain with high winds. | |

# WAR DIARY
## or
## INTELLIGENCE SUMMARY
*(Erase heading not required.)*

Army Form C. 2118.

| Place | Date | Hour | Summary of Events and Information | Remarks and references to Appendices |
|---|---|---|---|---|
| ALLERY | 24th March 1917 | | Promotions & Appointments | |

45272 Corp. T. Harn appts a/Lance Sergeant 22.3.17 Vice Harn evacuated.
30904 Lance Corp. W. Waldron Promoted a/Corpl. 1.3.17 Vice Allan to Base.
20907 a/Corp. W. Waldron to Corporal vice Allen to U.K. 12.3.17.
4146 Sgt. Chapman W. to Corporal 1.3.17 vice Hughes to France.
20907 L. Corp. W. Murphy to a/Corp. 6.3.17 vice Fanning to Lance Corporal.
20965 L/Corp. R. Wild to paid Lance Corp. 14.2.17 vice Vine to U.K.
7,9252 Pte. Stott. M. to paid Lance Corp. 10.3.17 vice Lurcell to U.K.
20476 Lce. Sergt. E. Murphy to Sergeant 1.3.17 vice McGrath to U.K.
45572 A/L Sgt. L. Harn to Lance Sergeant (Paid) vice Murphy promoted 1-3-17.

Work P.T., Drill, Rifle Ex., Gun Instruction & Classes.
Lecture by Lieut. J. H. Orpen "Machine guns in the attack".

Weather — Snow & Rain Showers.

# WAR DIARY
## or
## INTELLIGENCE SUMMARY

Army Form C. 2118.

| Place | Date | Hour | Summary of Events and Information | Remarks and references to Appendices |
|---|---|---|---|---|
| ALLERY | 25th March 1917 | | Church Parade. - Commanding Officer attended at CAVILLON for a Divisional Conference - by General Sir H. de B. Lisle. Subject "Open warfare" - | |
| | 26th March | | Divisional Field day - "The Division in the attack" to Easter Fri tot Gld. | |
| | 27th March | | Brigade Field day "The Brigade in Advance Guard" Weather - Snow & hail. | |
| | 28th March | | Work- P.D. Drill & Rifle Exercises. Digging in (New test) Packing of Limbers for Alert. The Commanding Officer delivered a Lecture at the 40th Divisional School. Subject - History of Machine Guns. Formation of Machine Gun Companies. Tactical Employment of Machine Guns. to Esther, 'Guy, Jini ——— | |

Army Form C. 2118.

# WAR DIARY
## or
## INTELLIGENCE SUMMARY

*(Erase heading not required.)*

Instructions regarding War Diaries and Intelligence Summaries are contained in F. S. Regs., Part II. and the Staff Manual respectively. Title Pages will be prepared in manuscript.

| Place | Date | Hour | Summary of Events and Information | Remarks and references to Appendices |
|---|---|---|---|---|
| ALLERY | 29th March 1917 | | The Company moved by march route to YZEUX and billeted into Billets to Batta. Showery. | |
| YZEUX | 30th March | | The Company halted for the day at this village. Repacking Limbers, Cleaning Guns, & Bathing. Weather fine. | |
| HALLOY | 31st March | | Moved by march route to billets at HALLOY. The marching of the Company too form good, no men having fallen out on the march. Weather: fine. Strength of Company last day of the month 10 officers 165 O.R.'s. | |

1st April 1917

E.C. Shifkwafe.
~~Crowle~~ 86 Co. Machine Gun Company.

**CONFIDENTIAL**

War Diary

of

86th Company, Machine Gun Corps.

Volume XIV.

From 1st April 1917 to 30th April 1917.

# WAR DIARY
## or
## INTELLIGENCE SUMMARY

Army Form C. 2118.

VOL XIV.

56th Machine Gun Company

| Place | Date Hour | Summary of Events and Information | Remarks and references to Appendices |
|---|---|---|---|
| HALLOY | 1st April 1917 | The Company moved by march route from HALLOY to GEZAINCOURT and billeted for the night. Weather cold and dull with hail & rain. | |
| GEZAINCOURT | 2nd April | Moved by train to billets at POMERA via DOULLENS. Weather strong winds and snow. | |
| | 3rd April | Route march approx distance 12 miles judging distance from church on the road. Weather bright & sunny. | |
| | 4th April | Intransit digging. Weather cold & sleet snow all day. | |
| | 5th April | Company marched to billets at OPPY arriving about 6 p.m. The Company was to inspected on the line of march by the Corps Commander (Lieut. Gen. Sir. J. Horne) who expressed satisfaction on the appearance of the Company. Capt. Frankfort, N.C.O's Elliott and Martin |  |

Army Form C. 2118.

# WAR DIARY
## or
## INTELLIGENCE SUMMARY

(Erase heading not required.)

Instructions regarding War Diaries and Intelligence Summaries are contained in F. S. Regs., Part II. and the Staff Manual respectively. Title Pages will be prepared in manuscript.

| Place | Date | Hour | Summary of Events and Information | Remarks and references to Appendices |
|---|---|---|---|---|
| OPPY | 6th April 1917 | | The Company Chinese Gong & equipment to Br. Bates. Packing limbers Judging distance and Bombing carried out. Weather Bright during morning noon. Heavy rain during evening night | |
| | 7th April | | The Company marched to WARLUZEL and billeted there. Drill and rifle exercises during the afternoon. Weather Bright. | |
| WARLUZEL | 8th April | | Company moved by march route to HUMBERCAMP and went into billets. Weather Bright and sunny. Snow during the night. | |
| | 9th April 10th " | | Drill and Rifle exercises. Gun drill & packing limbers | |

Army Form C. 2118.

# WAR DIARY
## or
## INTELLIGENCE SUMMARY

(Erase heading not required.)

Instructions regarding War Diaries and Intelligence Summaries are contained in F. S. Regs., Part II. and the Staff Manual respectively. Title Pages will be prepared in manuscript.

| Place | Date 1917 | Hour | Summary of Events and Information | Remarks and references to Appendices |
|---|---|---|---|---|
| SIMENCOURT | 11th April | | The Company moved by march route from HUMBERCAMP and went into Hutments at SIMEN COURT. A heavy fall of snow prevailing the whole march. | |
| | 12th April | | The march was continued to ARRAS where we arrived about 3pm and took billets in the CITADEL for the night. | |
| ARRAS | 13th April | | The Company received orders to occupy trenches in the recently taken German front at TILLOY. The Company marched out of the CITADEL at about 7am. arriving at TILLOY about 10 am and there occupied the former Captured trenches for the night. | |
| TILLOY | 13th April | | Operation Orders received for two Sections of the Company to relieve the 9th Machine Gun Company under orders of the G.O.C. 87th Infantry Brigade. No 1 & 3 Sections were detailed for this relief, they were attached respectively to (8C1 Sector) K.O.S.B.Y (N°3 Section) S.W. Borders. They occupied positions with their right on the COJEUL RIVER and their left 150 yards N. of the CAMBRAI ROAD. | |

# WAR DIARY
## or
## INTELLIGENCE SUMMARY

Army Form C. 2118.

| Place | Date | Hour | Summary of Events and Information | Remarks and references to Appendices |
|---|---|---|---|---|
| TILLOY | 1917 14th April | | Two Battalions of the Brigade were placed at the disposal of the G.O.C. 88th Brigade with the remaining two sections of the 86th Machine Gun Company. The Battalions and Gun Sections occupied positions in Strong Points on CHAPEL and ORANGE HILLS at about 4 p.m. The Company Headquarters being situate near FEUCHY CHAPELLE in the WANCOURT – FEUCHY Line. Weather continues Snow + Rain. | |
| FEUCHY | 15th April | | Nos 1 & 3 sections were withdrawn from the 87th Brigade and occupied positions on ORANGE HILL north of the CAMBRAI ROAD in relief of N° 2 & 4 section who had been pushed forward into MONCHY. -1A- PREUX to relieve the Gun Sections of the 88th Brigade. MONCHY to badly shelled and casualties are numerous. Weather Very Bad rendering work very difficult. | |

Army Form C. 2118.

# WAR DIARY
## or
## INTELLIGENCE SUMMARY
(Erase heading not required.)

Instructions regarding War Diaries and Intelligence Summaries are contained in F. S. Regs., Part II. and the Staff Manual respectively. Title Pages will be prepared in manuscript.

| Place | Date | Hour | Summary of Events and Information | Remarks and references to Appendices |
|---|---|---|---|---|
| MONCHY -LA- PREUX | 1917 16th April | | The Sixteen Guns of the Company are now employed in the line viz 1 & 3 on Orange Hill and 2 & 4 in MONCHY. One Gun was destroyed on ORANGE HILL by Shell fire causing 2 Casualties among the teams. Privates Warner and Harrison. Heavy shelling by the enemy of MONCHY village continues, and Casualties among the units are frequent. Weather Rain. | |
| | 17th April | | One Gun with No 3 Team was Knocked out. Pres. MERLIN & Archer. Shelling on Both sides very constant. | |
| | 18th April | | C.O. made a reconnaissance of MONCHY with a view of putting in more Machine Guns for the impending operations that are likely to take place and the grid positions where sites for Do Guns. The following casualty of No 3 Section occurred. Pte Davis wounded. Weather Still dry. | |

**Army Form C. 2118.**

# WAR DIARY
## or
## INTELLIGENCE SUMMARY
*(Erase heading not required.)*

| Place | Date | Hour | Summary of Events and Information | Remarks and references to Appendices |
|---|---|---|---|---|
| MONCHY -LA- PREUX | 1917 19th April | | Warning operation orders received, that the advance would be continued on the 22nd. 4th Machine Guns and two Regiments of each of the 86th & 88th Brigades would be employed in the operation, with other Divisions on our Right and Left. Two Casualties occurred in N section. Sergeant Doyle killed and Pte Fielder wounded. Weather. Dark but overcast. | |
| | 20th April | | Operation notified for 22nd now postponed until 23rd inst. | |
| | 21st April | | The enemy Division reported to be holding the front between LeCOJEUL RIVER and the SCARPE RIVER on the 3rd Bavarian Division (114th 18th & 23rd Bavarian Regts) on the South, and the 17th Division (7th Reserve) 163rd and 162nd Reserve Regts. Possibly by the 4th Bavarian Divisions. The advance will be continued on the 23rd April as a zero time to be notified later. | |

Army Form C. 2118.

# WAR DIARY
## or
## INTELLIGENCE SUMMARY

(Erase heading not required.)

Instructions regarding War Diaries and Intelligence Summaries are contained in F. S. Regs., Part II. and the Staff Manual respectively. Title Pages will be prepared in manuscript.

| Place | Date | Hour | Summary of Events and Information | Remarks and references to Appendices |
|---|---|---|---|---|
| MONCHY-LE-PREUX | 3rd April | | The Objectives of the 29th Division will be as follows— | |
| | | | 1st Objective (Blue line) | |
| | | | COPSE at O.8.B.12. (inclusive) — O.2. Central — T.32.c.8.4. | |
| | | | 2nd Objective (Red line) | |
| | | | O.9.d.5.1. — O.3.d.5.0. — O.3.d.2.8. Eastern edge of BOIS du SART. T.33.d.8.3. | |
| | | | The 88th Brigade will attack on the Right and a brigade of the 17th Division on the left. | |
| | | | The boundaries will be as follows.— between 87th & 88th Bdes. | |
| | | | East and West grid line between O.1. and O.7. | |
| | | | Between 87th Brigade and Brigade of 17th Division | |
| | | | T.31.c.2.3. — T.33.d.6.8 — T.34.a.0.6. | |
| | | | Between 88th Brigade and 15th Division | |
| | | | An East and West line from N.12. Central to O.9. Central and | |

| Place | Date | Hour | Summary of Events and Information | Remarks and references to Appendices |
|---|---|---|---|---|
| MONCHY -LE- PREUX | 1917 23rd April | | After the capture of the BLUE LINE the Divisional Artillery will move into previously prepared forward positions to assist the advance against the RED LINE. There will be a short Lull known after the capture of the BLUE LINE to enable the Artillery to move forward. The 88th Brigade will be in reserve with Hd qrs @ H.34.Central. The Lancashire Fusiliers and the Middlesex Regiment will be in the BROWN LINE and take over the defence of MONCHY north of the GRID LINE between O.1. and O.7.6. O.1.6.56. 7½ hours after Zero. The Dividing line between Battalions will be O.1.d.6.7.6.0.1.d.07. Both Battalion Headquarters will be at O.1.b.3.9. The Royal Fusiliers and Royal Dublin Fusiliers will move up to the BROWN LINE and will commence to occupy the trenches | |

**Place:** MONCHY-LE-PREUX

**Date:** Monday 21st April

**Hour:** Continued

vacated by the Middlesex Regt and Lancashire Fusiliers respectively by Bde this xxxx and half. They will relieve the troops holding the Divisional front on the night of the day following the Assault.

Artillery Preparation

The Heavy Artillery bombardment will commence 21st 10 p.m.

Artillery Barrage

The attack will be cover by an Artillery Barrage

Machine Guns

The Assault will be also covered by a Machine Gun Barrage. There will be 2 main Barrages, which will be referred to through the scheme as "A" and "B".

"A". A moving barrage to cover the advance of the Infantry developing into a standing barrage to cover the Consolidation

# WAR DIARY or INTELLIGENCE SUMMARY

Army Form C. 2118.

| Place | Date | Hour | Summary of Events and Information | Remarks and references to Appendices |
|---|---|---|---|---|
| MONCHY -LE- PREUX | 23rd April 1917 | | of the 1st Objective. To open on a N. & S. line from O.8.Central to O.2. to O.7. at Zero, remaining on this line until Zero plus 8 mins. At O. plus 8 minutes, O. plus 16 mins. O. plus 24 mins. there will be a lift of 200 yds until the final barrage line is all. and S. line from O.9.a.6.0. to I.33.c.0.6. 3. A protective barrage in front of the 2nd Objective on a N. & S. line from O.10. Central to I.34.Central. Grouping of Guns 58 H. M. 9.60 (1) A group of 19 guns at N.12. to 8.8. to open fire at 3Hrs and carry out the Barrage "A" remaining on the final barrage line of the 1st Objective until O plus 7 hours. | |

# WAR DIARY or INTELLIGENCE SUMMARY

Army Form C. 2118.

| Place | Date | Hour | Summary of Events and Information | Remarks and references to Appendices |
|---|---|---|---|---|
| MONCHY -LE- PREUX | 23rd April 1917 | | At O.Pip 6 hours heavy barrage of the Group move forward to the SUNKEN ROAD about O.8.c. 6. O.7.b. and carry out barrage "B" from D.10. central to O.4.d.05. The other Div. guns remain on the final barrage of the 1st objective until O.pip 7 hours. They then cease fire and move up to positions on the 1st objective and will be prepared to open on to barrage "B" should they be required. Owing to casualties please any O.M. guns detailed for this purpose out of action. (2) A group of 4 mobile guns to be in the Southern end of Jumping off trench at Zero. To follow the 2nd wave of Infantry and come up to positions about O.8. central and to central by direct fire the road and trenches in O.14.a. when not masked by our Infantry and at O.pip 7 hours to advance to 2nd objective in rear of Infantry and to engage such targets as may appear. | |

# WAR DIARY OR INTELLIGENCE SUMMARY

Army Form C. 2118.

| Place | Date | Hour | Summary of Events and Information | Remarks and references to Appendices |
|---|---|---|---|---|
| MONCHY -LE- PREUX | 23rd April 1917 | | 81st M.G. Company | |

(1) A group of 4 guns about O.1.b.9.3. Target, valley in T.33.c. Central. Range not less than 1500 yards. To fire from Zero to O. plus 32 minutes. At O. plus 32 minutes to lift 200 yards, remaining on final barrage line of 1st objective until O. plus 7 hours, when group ceases fire and moves up into 1st objective and carries out Barrage "B" from I.34.d.0.0. to I.34.b.0.0.

(2) A group of 4 guns about O.1.c.9.2. Target, Valley in O.7.d. – SUNKEN ROAD and ruined Mill at O.8.a. and c. – Cottage in O.8.b. To fire direct when not masked by our infantry, from Zero. at O. plus 32 minutes to lift on to final barrage line of 1st objective. To cease fire at O. plus 7 hours, and then move up to 1st objective and carry out Barrage "B" from O.10. central to O.4.d.0.5.

# WAR DIARY or INTELLIGENCE SUMMARY

Army Form C. 2118.

| Place | Date | Hour | Summary of Events and Information | Remarks and references to Appendices |
|---|---|---|---|---|
| MONCHY -LE- PREUX | 21st April 1917 | | 3. A group of 4 Mobile guns. To be in the Northern end of the "Jumping off" trench at 3.30. To follow 2nd wave of Infantry and take up a position about the COPSE O.2.a.2.5. 2 guns to control by direct fire the valley in T.33.c and two guns the valley in T.33.c. when not masked by our Infantry. As soon after the Capture of the 1st objective to work forward as close to our Artillery Standing barrage as possible and to control by direct fire the valley in T. 33.c Central, and the Bois du Sart. These guns advance to 2nd Objective in rear of Infantry and engage such targets as may appear. 56th M.G. Company A group of M.G. 8 guns, 4 of 86th and 4 of 189th M.G. Co. under O.C. 56th M.G. Co. at about N.6.d. Target Valley O.9.c. - Bois du Sart - Bois-du-Sart. To cease fire at Objective. De+guns of 89th Company & then M.G. ... at 2nd Objective and reinforce barrage B line as required. | |

Army Form C. 2118.

# WAR DIARY
## or
## INTELLIGENCE SUMMARY
*(Erase heading not required.)*

Instructions regarding War Diaries and Intelligence Summaries are contained in F. S. Regs, Part II. and the Staff Manual respectively. Title Pages will be prepared in manuscript.

| Place | Date | Hour | Summary of Events and Information | Remarks and references to Appendices |
|---|---|---|---|---|
| MONCHY -LE-PREUX | 21st April 1917 | | (1) Remainder of 16 M. Guns in Reserve - 8 of these to move forward after Capture of 1st Objective to MONCHY and take over Position vacated by 87th M.G.Co. <br><br> The guns detailed to advance at O plus 7 hours to that objective will only move forward when the Officer in Charge has satisfied himself that the advance from the Blue to the RED line has commenced). <br><br> Regiments Attacking <br> 87th Bde { Y/K.O.S.B. <br> { Y/R. Innis. Fus. <br> 88th Bde { Hants Regt. <br> { Worcester Regt. | |
| | 22nd April | | In accordance with the above operation orders. Emplacements were prepared in the Vicinity of M.6.d. Ammunition Dumps made and filled. Belt filling Rollers made. Tripods dug in, Angles of fire & direction carefully worked out. Officers and Gun Nos instructed in their respective Roles. | |

# WAR DIARY
## or
## INTELLIGENCE SUMMARY

Army Form C. 2118.

| Place | Date | Hour | Summary of Events and Information | Remarks and references to Appendices |
|---|---|---|---|---|
| MONCHY -LE- PREUX | 23rd April | | "Z" day for "Z" day (23rd April) It 4:45 a.m. the morning with a heavy grey mist which continued throughout the morning until nearly mid-day thus making observation extremely difficult. The weather otherwise was all that could be desired. Fine with slight W'ly wind. The guns of the 8th Co. were allotted as follows:— No.9 Section (4 guns) under Lieut. K.M. MOIR and A.H. HOSEGOOD and 4 guns of the 87th M.G.Co. under Lieut J. GREEN AT N.6.d. No.1 and No.3 Sections under Lieuts. J.H. ORPEN, & R. STREET in Reserve at ORANGE HILL ready to move forward to occupy positions vacated in front of MONCHY by the 87th Brigade. No.4 Section in support positions on ORANGE HILL to two guns mounted as A.A. Guns. At 4.45 a.m. the attack was launched on the whole Corps front in conjunction with the Corps on either side. | |

| Place | Date | Hour | Summary of Events and Information | Remarks and references to Appendices |
|---|---|---|---|---|
| MONCHY-LE-PREUX | 23rd April 1917 | | The 29th Division gained its 1st Objective, but the left Division was held up by Machine Gun Fire, and the Right Division, after advancing to the Foot of GUEMAPPA, was forced by a heavy Counter-attack to withdraw. The Corps on either flank were also subjected to heavy Counter attacks. The 4th Army on our left captured GAVRELLE. The following prisoners were despatched into the Corps Cage :— <br><br> 1. Officer <br> 76. O. Ranks <br><br> During the afternoon a fire was seen in VIS-EN-ARTOIS. <br><br> At about 10 a.m. Information was received from O.C. 87th M.G.Co. that the 1st Objective had been taken. The 8 guns in Reserve at ORANGE HILL were ordered to take up positions in front of MONCHY by 12 noon. A message was received from Lieut ORPEN that this had been carried out. | |

Army Form C. 2118.

# WAR DIARY
## or
## INTELLIGENCE SUMMARY
*(Erase heading not required.)*

Instructions regarding War Diaries and Intelligence Summaries are contained in F.S. Regs., Part II. and the Staff Manual respectively. Title Pages will be prepared in manuscript.

| Place | Date | Hour | Summary of Events and Information | Remarks and references to Appendices |
|---|---|---|---|---|
| MONCHY -LE- PREUX | 23rd April 1917 | | Firing was continued throughout the morning until 0 plus 7 hours, but as the advance to the 2nd Objective did not take place, firing was reduced to 4 shells per hour throughout the day. All guns remained in position throughout the day and night 23rd - 24th | |
| | 24th April | 8 a.m. | At 8 a.m. the following orders were received. 1. The 86th Brigade will attack the RED LINE to day 24K. from 0.9.6.5.1. – 0.3.d.2.9. – along Eastern edge of the BOIS-du-SART – I.33.d.9.6. 2. The attack will be carried out as follows:- Royal Fusiliers on the right – Dublin Fusiliers in the Centre – Lancashire Fusiliers on the left – Middlesex in Reserve. 3. Boundaries Between 86th Brigade and 15th Division. At this morning through N.12 Central – 0.7. Central thence to 0.9.6.5.1. | |

Wt. W14957/Mgo 750,000 1/16 J.B.C. & A. Forms/C.2118/12.
2449

**Army Form C. 2118.**

# WAR DIARY
## or
## INTELLIGENCE SUMMARY

*(Erase heading not required.)*

Instructions regarding War Diaries and Intelligence Summaries are contained in F. S. Regs., Part II. and the Staff Manual respectively. Title Pages will be prepared in manuscript.

| Place | Date | Hour | Summary of Events and Information | Remarks and references to Appendices |
|---|---|---|---|---|
| MONCHY -LE- PREUX | 24th April 1917 | | Between Royal Fusiliers and Dublin Fusiliers. Grid line between O.1 and O.7. — along line to between O.3 and O.9 including the whole of the BOIS-du-VERT and 100 yards N. of J. to Royal Fusiliers. Between Dublins and Lancashire Fusiliers. Line running through O.1 Central to O.3 Central, including Southern edge of the BOIS du SART to Royal Dublin Fusiliers. Between Lancashire Fusiliers and 51st Brigade. I.31.c.2.3. to I.33.d.9.8. # The 87th Brigade will hold the defences of MONCHY as far South as the Divisional boundary and PICK and STRING TRENCHES. 5 Artillery Barrage at 4 pm. | |

Army Form C. 2118.

# WAR DIARY
## or
## INTELLIGENCE SUMMARY

*(Erase heading not required.)*

Instructions regarding War Diaries and Intelligence Summaries are contained in F. S. Regs., Part II. and the Staff Manual respectively. Title Pages will be prepared in manuscript.

| Place | Date | Hour | Summary of Events and Information | Remarks and references to Appendices |
|---|---|---|---|---|
| MONCHY -LE- PREUX | 23rd April 1917 | 6 | Zero will be 4 p.m. | |
| | | 7 | Flank Divisions are making Simultaneous attacks | |
| | | 8 | The attack will be covered by machine gun Barrage as laid down for "B" Barrage. | |
| | | | (a) The 86th Machine Gun Co. will put in 8 guns to help thicken the Barrage. | |
| | | | (b) Eight guns will be detailed as Mobile guns replacing those of the 87th & 88th as laid in Scheme. | |
| | | 9 | A Contact Aeroplane will be in the Air. | |

| Place | Date | Hour | Summary of Events and Information | Remarks and references to Appendices |
|---|---|---|---|---|
| MONCHY -LE- PREUX | 24th April 1917 | | Disposition of Guns: I.R.M.G.C. <br><br> 4 Guns (Hotchkiss) under Lieut. J. ORPEN to accompany Royal Fusiliers <br> 4 Guns (Vickers) under Lieut. J.R. STREET to accompany Lancaster Fusiliers <br> 8 Guns for thickening in SHRAPNEL TRENCH, under Lieut. LEWIS HOOSE & WILLIAMS. <br><br> The attack was not successful, the RED LINE not being taken. The Vickers Guns only being able to get forward 300 to 400 yards. <br><br> At 11 pm. Orders were received that the Division would be relieved by the 3rd Division. <br><br> The No. M.G.Co. being relieved by the 16th M.G.C. | |
| | 25th April | | Nos 2, 3 & 4 Sections completed their reliefs by 3 pm and marched to ARRAS, and from there were conveyed by BUSSES | |

# WAR DIARY
## or
## INTELLIGENCE SUMMARY
*(Erase heading not required.)*

Army Form C. 2118.

| Place | Date | Hour | Summary of Events and Information | Remarks and references to Appendices |
|---|---|---|---|---|
| ARRAS | 25th April 1916 | | to BERNVILLE. No 1 Section were not able to be relieved until 10 pm. they marched to ARRAS and billeted for the night. | |
| BERNVILLE | 26th April | | The Company moved by march route to WANQUENTIN and was joined there by No 1 section. | |
| WANQUENTIN | 27th April | | The Company resumed the march to SOUASTRE. | |
| SOUASTRE | 28th to 30th April | | The Company was reequipped clothed & Bathed. Guns & Equipment Completely overhauled. All damaged Guns and parts repaired and New parts drawn from I.A.D.O.S. The total Casualties for the time in the Line Being:— 1 Officer (Lt. R Street) Killed. 1 Officer (Lieut. A.D.R.) Wounded. 8 O.R. Killed & 29 Wounded | |

# WAR DIARY or INTELLIGENCE SUMMARY

Army Form C. 2118.

| Place | Date | Hour | Summary of Events and Information | Remarks and references to Appendices |
|---|---|---|---|---|
| SCOASTRE | 30th April 1917 | | A draft of 2 Officers and 39 O.Ranks posted from the Base. | |

Strength of Company on 30th.

10 Officers
157 O.Ranks

Points of note observed during the Engagement:

(a) The want of men from Infantry units as Ammunition Carriers.

(b) An Extra water bottle filled with water for Gun until a Supply Can be got up.

(c) Ammunition Belts & Boxes found on the field can be filled with our own Ammunition and form an excellent Reserve.

GOUY-EN-ARTOIS
1st MAY 1917.

E.P. Schinkwin Major
Comdg 51 Coy. Machine Gun Corps

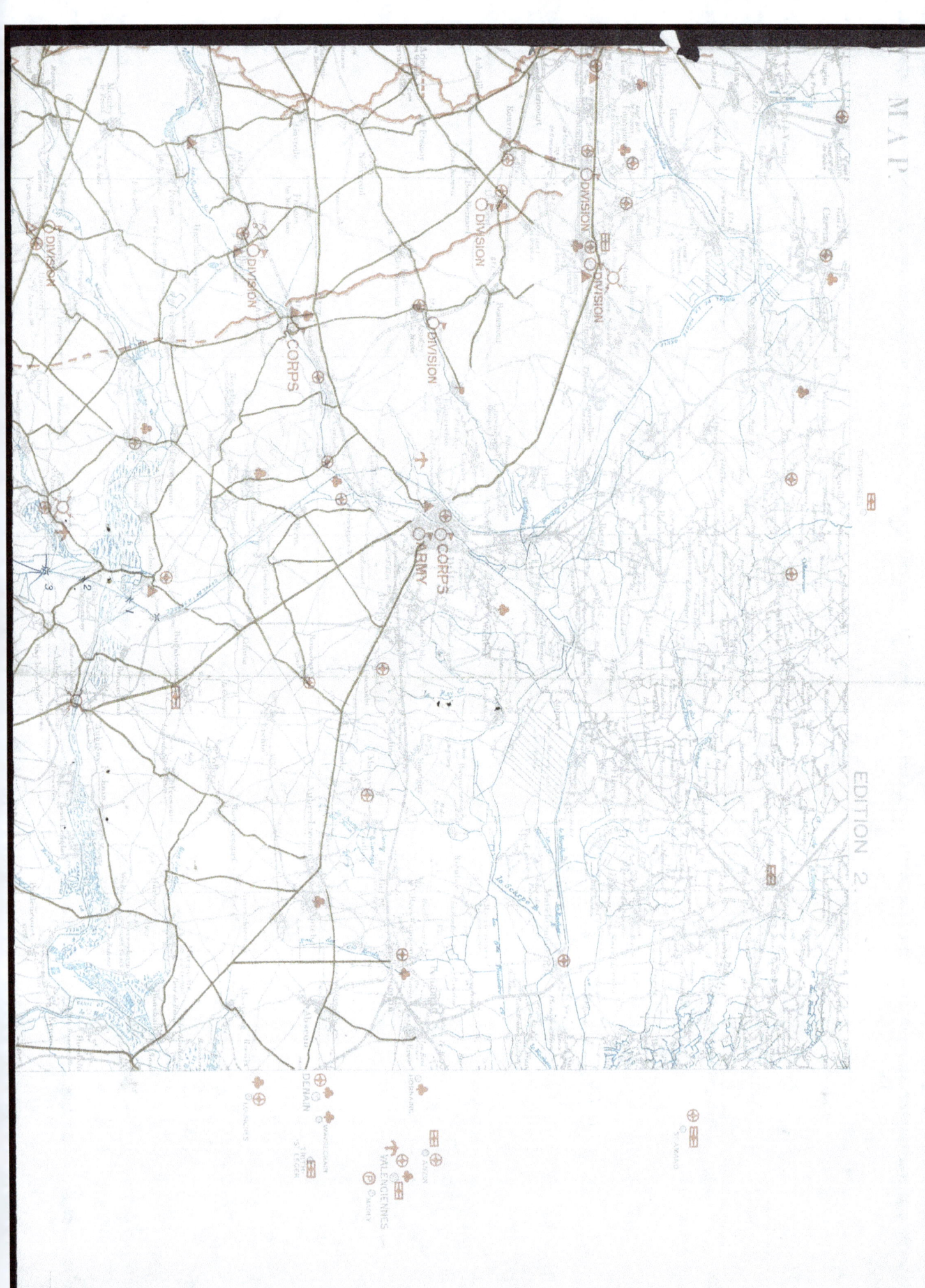

Vol 15

## Confidential

## War Diary of

## 86th Company, Machine Gun Corps

From 1st May 1917 To 31st May 1917

Volume XV

Army Form C. 2118.

# WAR DIARY
## or
## INTELLIGENCE SUMMARY.

Vol. XV. (Erase heading not required.)

86th Machine Gun Company.

| Place | Date 1917 | Hour | Summary of Events and Information | Remarks and references to Appendices |
|---|---|---|---|---|
| SOUASTRE | 1st May | | The Company moved by march route from SOUASTRE to GOUY-EN-ARTOIS and billeted for the night in huts. Weather. Brilliant sunshine. | |
| GOUY-EN-ARTOIS | 2nd May | | Road and Rifle exercises during the morning. Ropes pitches in the afternoon. The Company moved by road to ARRAS arriving there about 11-30 p.m. and proceeded to billets. Weather. Brilliant sunshine. Very hot. | |
| ARRAS | 3rd May | | The Company taken by motor on tour notice the huts being occupied by clearing rubbish from the billets which was found in a very dirty condition. No enemy fired aerial shells which fell in close proximity to the billets. Weather. Brilliant sunshine. Very hot. | |
| | 4th May | | A section of the company were employed clearing rubbish & debris from billets and roads in vicinity of billets. The remainder carried out a programme of work which included gun drills, stoppages and gun instruction. No enemy again shelled ARRAS. Weather. Brilliant sunshine. Very hot. | |
| | 5th May | | Church Parades. 3 hours notice cancelled. Weather. Brilliant sunshine. Very hot. | |
| | 6th May | | The Company carried out a programme of work which included gun drill, instruction and stoppages on the range, also coming into action for open warfare. An ammunition dump was exploded at ST CATHERINE which caused many casualties. Took Reeges. Weather. Brilliant sunshine. | |

(A7050) Wt. W12539/M1293 750,000. 1/17. D.D. & L., Ltd. Forms/C.2118/14.

# WAR DIARY
## or
## INTELLIGENCE SUMMARY.

(Erase heading not required.)

Army Form C. 2118.

Instructions regarding War Diaries and Intelligence Summaries are contained in F.S. Regs., Part II. and the Staff Manual respectively. Title pages will be prepared in manuscript. 86th Machine Gun Company. Vol. IV.

| Place | Date | Hour | Summary of Events and Information | Remarks and references to Appendices |
|---|---|---|---|---|
| ARRAS. | 7th May. | | The Company carried out the usual programme as for the day previous. 2nd Lieut. W. Wilkes from Base joined the Company. The Corps Commander awarded Military Medals to the undermentioned for acts of gallantry during the recent operations:— 20901 Cpl. Walden (wounded) 20030. Pte. H. Gott (wounded) called ARMS.M. to wounds to the Sgt. killed. The enemy's high velocity gun shelled ARRAS in the vicinity during night. Bright hot. Heavy rain during night. Weather. | |
| | 8th May. 9th May. | | The Company marched to DAINVILLE where a good billet was obtained. In the afternoon Lewis gun classes were carried on. Lt. Sergeants & Corporals were instructed in Lewis gun firing. Gun teams by Nos. & combine. He high velocity gun shelled a part in the officers' Mess wounding Pte. E. Durden. Lewis gun teams. Heavy Rain & Thunder storm. | |
| | 10th May. | | Parades were carried out as for the day previous. The Company left the MONCHY road. The Enemy's Long Range Gun during the night and education morning."— The Robert wounded wounded morton missing believed wounded Carson attacked from 2nd Sigs. Two Aldridge wounded. Very warm. Brilliant sunshine. | |
| | 11th May. | | He Enemy were carried out and a Company to balloons but not arriving until ?am. The Company marched from ARRAS to DAINVILLE in the evening arriving about 8pm. and were billeted there. Capt. G.H. arrived. Weather. Brilliant sunshine. Very warm. | |

Army Form C. 2118.

# WAR DIARY
## or
## INTELLIGENCE SUMMARY.
*(Erase heading not required.)*

864 Machine Gun Company

Instructions regarding War Diaries and Intelligence Summaries are contained in F.S. Regs., Part II. and the Staff Manual respectively. Title pages will be prepared in manuscript.

Vol. XV.

| Place | Date | Hour | Summary of Events and Information | Remarks and references to Appendices |
|---|---|---|---|---|
| DAINVILLE | 12th May. | | The Company paraded in drill shoes owing to the lear caused on the leather uppers of marching boots and over rough ground retained in manœuvre. Two guns were mounted at DAINVILLE Ammunition Dump to protect it from hostile aircraft. The guns were under the supervision of an officer. Weather: Dulls & Showers. Stay warm. | |
| | 13th May. | | Church Parade. The Company was inspected by the G.O.C. 84th Brigade and received a good report on condition of equipment & appearance. Weather: Bright tender showers later. During the afternoon the band played at H.Q. 12th May. | |
| | 14th May. | | The gun teams tho came out of the line checked their packed number by the guns & ammunition was checked number preparatory to move to ARRAS. Weather: Fine & warm. | |
| | 15th May. | | The Company moved by march route to ARRAS. Arrived about 11.15 a.m. went in billets. M.G. teams were billeted with Infantry. Weather: Very Fine. | |
| ARRAS | 16th May. | | The Company paraded at 7 a.m. for Squad Drill under the Section Officers. After breakfast paraded in Fighting Order and marched to range. Bayonets worth stables, drill & rifle exercises were carried out. Attached men were employed in cleaning the billets. 9th Essex house were not into the line relieved 4 guns of 87th Essex in the pivot point No. 1 at MONCHY-LE-PREUX. The relief was carried out successfully. Weather: Good. Heavy rain during night. | |

Army Form C. 2118.

# WAR DIARY
## or
## INTELLIGENCE SUMMARY.

(Erase heading not required.)

Instructions regarding War Diaries and Intelligence Summaries are contained in F. S. Regs., Part II. and the Staff Manual respectively. Title pages will be prepared in manuscript. 862 Machine Gun Coy. Vol. XV.

| Place | Date | Hour | Summary of Events and Information | Remarks and references to Appendices |
|---|---|---|---|---|
| ARRAS | 17th May | | The Company paraded at 7am for Physical Drill. After breakfast, paraded in fighting order and marched to RACE COURSE where advancing over rough ground, coming into action was carried out. In the afternoon a lecture on Sanitation was given by the Section Officer. | |
| | 18th May | | The Company paraded in Field order with tacks, shovels and overgear to the Old German front line where advance digging was carried out. By Coy. practiced to advance to occupying them. Drill with machine guns was also carried out. One section was sent out to reconnoitre gun positions in the line with a view to occupying them for the forthcoming operations. In the afternoon the remainder of Coy. were employed with cleaning guns and keeping them for the line. Nos 2 & 3 Sections were taken over & the line in the wing took up temporary posted positions to NORTH of MONCHY. | |
| | 19th May | | Weather fine & warm. No. 1 section was ordered to stand by ready employed in changing, repairing, guns for the Lewis. No 102 Division carried out an attack in accordance with attached order. | SO/18 Bn. Instruct Map. |
| | 20th May | | Fine weather. The Company relieved the 89th Coy. on the line the situation facing them apparently unconsolidated. Forward Heights with outposts in ORANGE HILL and the 10.0. rations were billeted in the LEWIS BARRACKS | |

Army Form C. 2118.

# WAR DIARY
## of
## INTELLIGENCE SUMMARY.
(Erase heading not required.)

Instructions regarding War Diaries and Intelligence Summaries are contained in F. S. Regs., Part II. and the Staff Manual respectively. Title pages will be prepared in manuscript.

| Place | Date | Hour | Summary of Events and Information | Remarks and references to Appendices |
|---|---|---|---|---|
| MONCHY | 21st May 19 17 | | The relief between the Companys was completed without incident. Enemy Artillery was active. MONCHY was heavily shelled between 8pm and 9pm. 7.30pm and 8pm. to 9pm. at about 6.45 am. 4 machine guns were very active from the N. machine guns edge of the Bois du SART. They were immediately engaged by our machine guns no further fire action has been observed from this direction. Snipers Enemy sniper was very busy at dawn from shell holes in front of HOOK TRENCH. Our Snipers replied vigorously and succeeded in quietening them. Aeroplanes Two hostile planes came over our line between 4.30am and 6am. Whenever an enemy patrol was observed, fire was opened upon them during the night and one was seen to fall. Enemy Signals It was observed that when the enemy's shells were falling short on DEVILS TRENCH, green flares were invariably fired from the trench and the range was lengthened. Weather: Hot & Dry. | |

# WAR DIARY
## or
## INTELLIGENCE SUMMARY.
(Erase heading not required.)

Army Form C. 2118.

| Place | Date | Hour | Summary of Events and Information | Remarks and references to Appendices |
|---|---|---|---|---|
| MONCHY | 1917 22 MAY | | Artillery. Below normal, during the evening BIT LANE and ARROW HEAD COPSE was rather heavily shelled and at dusk the area between SHRAPNEL and EAST TRENCH was shelled with SHRAPNEL. Machine Guns. Two machine guns in DEVIL TRENCH at about T.31.2.C.5.5. 10 lost action during the night, also the gun under CART in BIT LANE. Trench Mortars. a few light trench mortars were fired at S.W. corner of TWIN COPSE from a N.E. direction. Movement. Continual movement near HATCHET WOOD on our artillery shelling the area a number of the enemy were seen running in all directions. At 3 pm when some of our shells fell in no man's land at O.2.6.2.3.3 Germans with no arms or equipment were seen to jump up from Cross and run back into HOOK TRENCH. General. After our bombardment of D.5. FIVE TRENCH the enemy let lit four fires in his lines. These gave off clouds of smoke, having a sickly odour. Weather. Foot. | |

# WAR DIARY or INTELLIGENCE SUMMARY

Army Form C. 2118.

| Place | Date | Hour | Summary of Events and Information | Remarks and references to Appendices |
|---|---|---|---|---|
| MONCHY | 1917 23 MAY | | Enemy Artillery was quieter than usual. LANCER LANE was the only spot continuously shelled. It was noticed that the enemy used his field guns far more by night than by day. Machine Guns. Hostile machine guns again active in DEVILS TRENCH during the night. One at I.32.c.45.20 and the other near CIGAR COPSE. Also two fired from S.W. corner of BOIS des AUBEPINES. Our PATROLS. A patrol tried to enter DEVILS TRENCH but found it strongly held. Machine guns and Rifle fire were opened on them. HOOK TRENCH is held by a series of posts with 20 to 30 in each. AEROPLANES. Two enemy planes flew low over our lines at 4.30 p.m. and dropped Red and White lights N. of MONCHY. Two others with streamers on their planes approached our lines at about 4.10 a.m. firing the machine guns in reply to our fire. Movement during the day. Small parties of men were frequently seen moving about in the BOIS du SART. One machine gun fired on them. A Small party seen digging at I.32. c.3.4 were dispersed by machine gun fire. | |

Army Form C. 2118.

# WAR DIARY
or
## INTELLIGENCE SUMMARY
(Erase heading not required.)

| Place | Date | Hour | Summary of Events and Information | Remarks and references to Appendices |
|---|---|---|---|---|
| MONCHY | 1917 24 MAY | | Artillery The enemy shelled the neighbourhood of Battalion Hdqrs at O.1.a.7.9. Continually. This appears to be one of his registering points. About 100 shells fell during the day and night around LANCER LANE. MONCHY and the area to the W. & N.W. of the village was shelled. Machine Guns active during the night on HILL TRENCH, from direction of BOIS du VERT and BOIS des AUBEPINES. Aircraft at about 9 p.m. an enemy Bi-plane flew high over LANCER LANG and dropped a white light breaking into Stars, on which signal a short Shrapnel bombardment of the trench followed. 5 hostile Machines were driven off by our Machine Gun fire. Movements at 10 p.m. men were seen crossing a small dip in the ground at O.2.d. Central where earth appeared to be thrown up. Our Machine Guns opened fire. Light Signals every morning at about 5.45 a.m. the enemy sends up white lights from all along ANGEL and DEVILS TRENCH, possibly to denote his position. | |

Army Form C. 2118.

# WAR DIARY
## or
## INTELLIGENCE SUMMARY

*(Erase heading not required.)*

Instructions regarding War Diaries and Intelligence Summaries are contained in F. S. Regs., Part II. and the Staff Manual respectively. Title Pages will be prepared in manuscript.

| Place | Date | Hour | Summary of Events and Information | Remarks and references to Appendices |
|---|---|---|---|---|
| MONCHY | 1917 24 MAY | | SNIPERS increasing activity was shewn especially from BOIS des AUBE-PINE and from Shell holes in front of HOOK TRENCH. PATROLS Our Patrols report the Enemy holding DEVILS TRENCH Strongly held. | |
| | 25 MAY | | Artillery Brigade Headquarters at H.23.d.3.9. was shelled at intervals during the day. The Batteries N. & S.W. of MONCHY was shelled at 9 p.m. and 8 a.m. Machine Guns active during the night especially at O2.d.4.5. a Machine Gun was seen firing at intervals from about I.32.a.1.2. Snipers were active from Shell holes and bits of Trenches in front of BOIS des AUBEPINE. Our own Snipers made good use of opportunities in the early morning, to which the enemy replied with light Trench Mortars. Aircraft at about 5.40 a.m. 4 enemy Planes came over our lines. One was brought down and fell behind the enemy lines. | |

Army Form C. 2118.

# WAR DIARY
## or
## INTELLIGENCE SUMMARY
(Erase heading not required.)

Instructions regarding War Diaries and Intelligence Summaries are contained in F. S. Regs., Part II. and the Staff Manual respectively. Title Pages will be prepared in manuscript.

| Place | Date | Hour | Summary of Events and Information | Remarks and references to Appendices |
|---|---|---|---|---|
| MONCHY | 19/17 26th MAY | | Artillery during the morning of the 25th LONE and BAYONET TRENCHES were shelled, but most of the shells were duds. GRAPE and SHRAPNEL were shelled, also MONCHY and the Batteries W. & S.W. of the Village. VINE LANE received intermittent attention. Battalion Hdqrs at O.1.C.9.2. was shelled most of the night. Machine Guns Not so active. Snipers active at dusk. Aircraft Considerable activity on both sides at 8 p.m. 6 enemy planes with red bodies attacked and forced one of our machines down on ORANGE HILL. Two of the enemy's machines were brought down over their own lines. Enemy Movement Two enemy working parties were dispersed in front of HOOK TRENCH at dawn by machine gun fire. | |

# WAR DIARY
## or
## INTELLIGENCE SUMMARY

Army Form C. 2118.

| Place | Date | Hour | Summary of Events and Information | Remarks and references to Appendices |
|---|---|---|---|---|
| MONCHY | 27th MAY 16/17 | | **Artillery** Enemy. The area round MONCHY and Battery positions were heavily shelled at intervals during the afternoon. GRAPE, SHRAPNEL & DALE TRENCHES were heavily shelled but own Bombardment of DEVILS TRENCH, BOIS des AUBE PINES, BOIS du SART & WOOD TRENCH appeared to be very effective. **Machine Guns** a gun was firing between Midnight and 2am from DEVILS TRENCH. **Aircraft** at 5am this morning two enemy planes flew up and down our line at a low altitude. We engaged them with Lewis Guns & Vickers. 3 machines were brought down in their own lines one at 10am and two at 7.20pm. **Enemy Movement** During our bombardment at 5.55pm. 3 men were seen retiring from underneath the Cart in BIT LANE. This spot was kept under MACHINE gun and Rifle fire. A hostile wiring party in front of "C1 and C2" pos was dispersed by Machine gun fire. **Snipers** at 5.30pm there was a big explosion in ST ROHARTS FACTORY probably a Dump. | |

# WAR DIARY or INTELLIGENCE SUMMARY

Army Form C. 2118.

| Place | Date | Hour | Summary of Events and Information | Remarks and references to Appendices |
|---|---|---|---|---|
| MONCHY | 28th MAY 1917 | | **Artillery** Shelling round MONCHY was persistent all day. Shelling of the Right Sector was less active than usual. **Machine Guns** One gun fired on SHRAPNEL TRENCH from the BOIS DES AUBÉ - PINES. **Snipers** Quiet during the day, not active at dawn. Some enemy snipers are believed to be accounted for. **Movements** Parties were observed working on the GREEN WORK by day. During our bombardment of HOOK TRENCH four men were seen to jump out and run to a shell hole, they were unequipped. **Aircraft** A hostile plane flew over Battalion H.Q. at N.6.b.7.4. at 6.55 pm. and dropped a Red and green light, which was the signal for a bombardment of the particular spot with 5.9's. | |
| | 29th May | | **Artillery** Our Left Brigade area came in for a steady shelling during the morning, and at 9 p.m. the enemy opened an intense barrage of 7.4's and h'kiz, bangs which lasted for 15 minutes. In our Sector the day was quiet. **Machine Guns** 3 guns were active from DEVIL'S TRENCH. **Aeroplanes** Our planes were active all day. Several hostile planes flying by our battle planes crossed our lines, but were driven back. | |

2449 Wt. W14957/M90 750,000 1/16 J.B.C. & A. Forms/C.2118/12.

| Place | Date | Hour | Summary of Events and Information | Remarks and references to Appendices |
|---|---|---|---|---|
| MONCHY | 29th MAY 1917 | | The usual movements were observed around HATCHET WOOD. SNIPERS at 4 a.m. this morning one of our Lewis Guns caught a party of 5 Germans leaving a Shell hole to go back to their trenches opposite T.31.b.5.6. 3 of the party were shot, and then our Lewis one of our Snipers claims to have hit a German officer who showed himself in DEVIL TRENCH. Two German Snipers were accounted for who were firing from Shell holes in front of ARROW TRENCH.  OPERATIONS Orders for an operation to be carried out night of 29/30 | See Oper: orders b/3 30.5. |
| | | | Copy of Orders attached | |
| | 30th May | | Result of Operations attacked. The Company was relieved in the line by the 87th M.G. Company. Casualties 2 Killed 9 wounded. Strength at End of Month 10 Officers 160. 149 O.R. | |

E.B. Smith Major
Comdg 86 G. Machine Gun Corps

1st June 1917

SECRET

**86th Brigade Order No 139**

Reference
attached MAP.

1. The 29th Division has been ordered to capture INFANTRY HILL and the BOIS DES AUBEPINES, in conjunction with the 56th Division, who will co-operate, and occupy those parts of LONG TRENCH and HOOK TRENCH, which lie within their area.

2. The 87th Infantry Brigade (with Headquarters at N.5.a. central) will attack the objectives shewn in RED and BLUE on the attached Map, on the evening of the 19th instant, at an hour Zero to be notified later.

    The 167th Infantry Brigade (with Headquarters at N.10.d.3.7.) will carry out the attack on that portion of the objective within the 56th Division area on the same date and hour.

3. The 86th Brigade will be in Divisional Reserve.
    The 16th Middlesex Regiment will occupy the BROWN LINE on the night of the 19th/20th May, as soon as it is vacated by the Border Regt. at present holding it.

    The remainder of the 86th Brigade will remain in ARRAS, ready to move at an hours notice.

4. The enemy troops reported to be holding the front between the RIVER SCARPE and the CAMBRAI ROAD are the 9th Reserve Division (19th, 6th and 395th Regiments) on the north, and the 36th Division (175th, 128th, and 5th Grenadier Regiments) on the south.

5. The attack will take place under an intense artillery barrage, which will open on the RED LINE at Zero. It will lift at Zero plus 4 minutes and advance at the rate of 50 yards a minute to the BLUE LINE from which it will lift at Zero plus 10 minutes.
    At Zero the troops will leave their trenches, and get as close to the barrage as possible in order to enter the enemys trench immediately the barrage lifts.

7. The assault will be covered by a Machine Gun barrage, details of which will be issued later.

cont.

SECRET

2.

## 86th Brigade Order No. 139.

8. At Zero hour "J" Special Coy R.E. will, if the wind is favourable discharge LIEVENS PROJECTORS on the BOIS DU VERT, and the Sunken Road O.3.c. North of the BOIS DU VERT.

9. At Zero hour No 1 Special Coy R.E. will barrage the trench from I.32.d.2.8. to I.32.a.0.7. and the valley beyond with Smoke Bombs from 4" Stokes Mortars.

10. The objectives will be consolidated as soon as they are captured, and posts with Lewis Guns will be pushed out to hold the Wood at O.2.d.9.5.

    Strong Points will be constructed at approximately the following places:-

    O.2.d.9.3. - O.2.d.9.8. - O.2.b.8.4. -
    O.2.b.6.9. - I.32.d.2.0. - I.32.c.2.4.

11. The advanced Dressing Station will be at N.5.a.6.3. with a combined Regimental Aid Post at N.6.d.6.2.

12. Stragglers Posts will be established by 87th Inf Brigade at the Cross Roads H.28.c.3.1. These Posts will be under the supervision of the A.P.M.

13. Prisoners will be sent to the Prisoners Cage, established at H.33.b.6.8. where they will be handed over to the A.P.M.

14. Units will send a representative to Brigade Headquarters at 10-0 a.m. and 6.p.m. on the 19th instant to synchronise watches.

SECRET.    29th Division No. C.G.S. 53/7.

29th Divisional Machine Gun Scheme issued in conjunction with
29th Division Order No 121 dated 17th May 1917.

1. **INFORMATION**

   (a) *The Enemy*

   At present holds the tactical point from which he secures his observation and which is disadvantageous to us.

   (b) *Own Troops.*

   87th Brigade — The Brigade as per margin will form the assaulting troops

   (c) The object of the attack is to improve the line already held by the Division but the chief aim is to gain tactical advantage in order to achieve observation

   (d) The Machine Guns of the Division will be utilised in order to form.
   1. Protective Barrage
   2. Local control of tactical points
   3. Prevent enemy movement
   4. To help consolidation
   5. Fire defensive flanks.

2. **INTENTIONS.** It is the intention of the G.O.C. to assault the enemy system of defence opposite the right Brigade Group and consolidate on the line as per attached map.

3. **DISTRIBUTION.** The 86th Company (Commander as margin) will provide 8 guns

   86th Coy (under Major Beckwith)
   87th Coy (under Major Burrill)     The 87th Company will furnish 16 guns
   88th Coy (under Major Morris)      The 88th Company will supply 14 guns.

4. **ALLOTTED.**
   POSITION AREAS FOR BARRAGE   The areas as allotted in this paragraph will be occupied 24 hours before Zero

   Over

## 4. ALLOTTED POSITION AREAS FOR BARRAGE

| Machine Gun Unit | No | Area Co-ordinates |
|---|---|---|
| The 86th Coy | 1 | H.36.b. |
| The 87th Coy | 2 | EAST.TRENCH O.7. Cnt O.1.b. to O.7.b. |
| The 88th Coy | 3 | I.19.c., I.31.d |

Gun Complement per Unit for Barrage

- 86th Company = 8 guns
- 87th Company = 11 guns
- 88th Company = 10 guns

## 5. BARRAGE ZONES

Zones to form the standing protective barrage, are definitely allotted the different adjacent contact fire limitations forming the complete barrage line.

| No of Guns | Company | Area | Barrage line |
|---|---|---|---|
| 8 | 86th | H.36.b. | O.3.a.60.60 to I.33.c.50.60 |
| 7 | 87th | O.1.b. to O.7.b. | O.9.a.7.1. to O.3.d.2.7 |
| 4 | " | O.7.b central | O.3.d.2.7. to O.3.b.1.2. |
| 4 | 88th | O.1.a.4.7 | O.3.b.1.2. to O.3.a.6.6 |
| 4 | " | I.25.c.2.3. | I.33.c Central to I.32.d.8.? |
| 2 | " | I.19.c. | I.32.d.8.9. to I.32.a.8.5. |

## 6. PRELIMINARY RECONNAISSANCE

All Officers will make a reconnaissance of their areas and give special attention to the following points.

a. Avenues of approach (own and enemy)
b. Backward and lateral communication
c. Forward tactical sites (in case of advance)
d. Ammunition dumps (seperate and well forward)
e. Assembly Points
f. Water Dumps
g. Visual Stations
h. Replenishment Shelters
i. Where minor repairs are to be effected in case of emergency
j. The position of the nearest telephone
k. The location of Brigade Headquarters
l. Position of Fighting Limbers
m. What guns are necessary for the protection of ones own front
n. What support can be expected from the guns of adjoining Machine Gun Units
o. The position of ones own immediate reserve
p. The defined limits of the advance
q. The nearest natural water supply
r. Range marks and the selection points

over

3

**6. PRELIMINARY RECONNAISSANCE**

    s. The artillery barrage zone
    t. The rate of progression
    u. The nearest dressing station
    v. The summit of the safety margin
    w. Forward observation posts
    x. Final dispositions to reap maximum fire effect
    y. Liaison with Infantry
    z. Determination of Zero and synchronisation of time.

**7. PROTECTIVE MEASURES.**

The 5 guns in SHRAPNEL Trench will not form part of the barrage complement but will remain in their present positions and go forward as mobile guns with the resulting troops taking up positions in the Strong Points as follows:-

    I. 32. 0. 2. 4.
    I. 32. d. 2. 0.
    O. 2. b. 6. 9.
    O. 2. b. 8. 4.
    O. 2. d. 9. 3.

They will be replaced by 4 guns of the 8 barrage guns in the vicinity of EAST Trench approximately. This simultaneous progression will be arranged for by the Officer Commanding the Machine Gun Unit of the Right Sector.

The Machine Guns of the Left Sector will remain in their Battle Emplacements with the following exceptions which will be required for barrage purposes:-

    4 guns in Strong Point move to I. 25. c. 2. 3.
    4 guns (SCABBARD Trench and MUSKET Trench
                            move to O. 1. a. 4. 7)
    2 guns ROEUX WOOD) will barrage from their emplacements by enfilade

**8. RESERVE AMMUNITION CACHES**

Must be established in the forward area on the basis of 15 boxes per gun. It is better to have several small dumps easily accessible than one main dump.

**9. FIRE REGISTRATION.**

Guns will render as far as possible avoiding too many guns firing at the same time which may arouse the suspicion of the enemy of the impending event.

**10. WATER SUPPLY**

The method already proved by experience to be practical will be adopted.
Each N.C.O going into action will take a full 2 gallon petrol tin of water in his pack.
Forward water dumps will be established

**11. COMMUNICATIONS**

Good communications in the present phase of war are one of the important factors of success.
(a) Visual Stations have previously failed but shutters should be taken forward in case suitable opportunity should arise.

4.

**11. COMMUNICATIONS**
   b. By telephone
   c. By runner. Intelligent personnel should be chosen.

**12. AMMUNITION SUPPLY**
Classified as follows:-
(a) Forward S.A.A. dumps
(b) Full gun complement of 14 boxes per gun
(c) Replenishment shelters.
(d) Bandolier method.
(e) Spare numbers to collect from casualties.
(f) Progressive supply, have S.A.A. limbers at fixed point at a stated time during the operations
(g) By chain of carriers.

**13. SPARE PARTS AND OIL.**
Detail special gun members for the carrying of spare parts and oil.

**14. PROGRESSIVE RANGE CARDS and KEY RANGES.**
Assume the occupation of regained territory and make range cards from the map.
Due allowance must be made for "The Error of The Day"

**15. DISPOSITION REPORTS**
Should be rendered as soon as possible with general direction of fire.
Find out the positions of guns on either flank to prevent wastage of fire energy.

**16. FIRE CONTROL**
Guns are grouped under the orders of a Fire Control Commander

**17. FIRE ACTION.**
From the moment the barrage falls.
Fire will be maintained for one and a half hours after Zero.

Appendix to 29th Division Order No 121.

The arrangements for the Artillery barrage are as follows:-
At Zero a barrage will be placed on the line A.B.C.D.E.
The fall of the barrage is the signal for the troops to leave the trenches; and at Zero, the troops advance from our front line, and get as close to the barrage as possible

If troops reach the barrage, before it commences to creep back, they should kneel down; they must not however lie down.

At 5 minutes after Zero (ie 0.5.) the barrage will lift 100 yards off the front line, thus enabling our troops to enter the enemy's front line trenches.

The barrage will creep back at the rate of 100 yards every two minutes, reaching the second objective at 0.7. and lifting off it at 0.10. From here, it will creep to the line H.J.K.L.E. at the rate of 100 yards every two minutes.

The barrage will continue on the line H.J.K.L.M in bursts for one hour (ie till O plus 1 hour 15 mins) to enable the troops to consolidate

Should the S.O.S. call (a succession of Red Very lights) be made, while our troops are consolidating the second objective, a barrage will be placed on the line H.J.K.L.M

# Artillery Barrage Map.

*14.5.17*

Secret.                                      No 2 op, order
                                              with map

## 86th Machine Gun Company
## Operation Order No 15
### by
### Major E. Beckwith. M.C.

Reference
Corps Trench Map 1/10.000.                27th May 1917.

1. **General Information**

    The 86th Infantry Brigade plus 8th Battn. East Lancashire Regt. lent by the 112th Infantry Brigade has been ordered to advance our line, and capture & consolidate Hook Trench and Tool Trench from O.2.b.4.0. to O.8.b.2.1.

2. **Method of Attack**

    The 18th Middlesex Regt on the left, the 1st Battn Lancashire Fusiliers in the centre, and the 8th East Lancashire Regiment on the right.

    Dividing lines between Battalions:-

    Between 18th Middlesex Regiment and 1st Lancashire Fusiliers

    A line drawn East and West from the Sap just North of Green Lane at O.2.d.1.3. (Sap inclusive to 1st Battalion Lancashire Fusiliers)

    Between 1st Lancashire Fusiliers and 8th Battn. East Lancashire Regiment.

    A line drawn East & West from Junction of Hill Trench and Grape Trench.

3. **Zero Hour**

    This hour will be notified later.

4. **The Assault**

    At Zero hour the assaulting troops will

will advance, and when within 20 yards of the objective, will rush the position.

### 5. Headquarters

Brigade N.5.a. central.

Battalions of the assaulting forces will move to the Dug Outs in Shrapnel Trench on the night of 29th/30th.

Machine Gun Company in the Machine Gun Emplacement under the Crucifix, Monchy.

### 6. Dressing Station

Advanced Dressing Station will be at N.5.a.5.3. with a combined aid post at N.6.d.5.2.

### 7. Prisoners

Prisoners will be sent to Corps Forward Cage and handed over to Corps A.P.M.

### 8. Watches

Watches will be synchronised at 6 p.m. on the day of the Assault.

### 9. Maps and Orders.

The Officer in command of the Mobile Section will not take over the Top with him any Maps shewing our own Trenches or dispositions. He will also warn his N.C.O.s and men that they must not take any papers or letters that would be useful to the Enemy.

### 10. Machine Guns

The Machine Guns of the Division will be distributed as follows:-

86th Company under Major E. Beckwith M.C.
18 Guns (to include 2 of 87th Company)

87th Company under Major H.R. Burrill
  12 Guns

88th Company under Major A. Morris
  16 Guns.

63rd Company.
  16 Guns

112th Company under Lieut. Tonks.
  4 Guns

11. Barrage Fire

A Barrage Fire will be put on:

| | |
|---|---|
| 4 Guns. | O.3.b.1.2. to O.3.a.6.6. |
| 4 Guns. | O.3.a.6.6. to I.33.c.5.6 |
| 2 Guns. | I.33.c. central to I.32.a.8.5. |
| 10. Guns. | O.3.b.1.2. to O.9.a.7.2. |

12. Gun Positions

The 14 Guns of the 86th Company in the Monchy defence and Shrapnel Trench, together with the guns of the 88th Company will remain in the present battle emplacements for the maintenance of the Barrage.

The following Guns in Monchy are allotted defined targets as shown

Line I.32.d.80.95 — I.33.c.55.65 — O.3.a.6.6.

| Gun | @ Position | Range | Co-ordinates of Targets. |
|---|---|---|---|
| H. | O.1.a.9.7 | 1900 | O.3.a.6.6. – O.3.a.6.9. |
| J. | O.1.b.2.5. | 1700 | O.3.a.6.9 – I.33.c.6.2. |
| K. | O.1.b.3.3. | 1750 | I.33.c.6.2 – I.33.c.55.65. |
| L. | O.1.d.2.9 | 1850 | I.33.c.55.65 – I.33.c.35.60. |
| M. | O.1.d.2.8. | 1800 | I.33.c.35.60 – I.33.c.15.75. |
| N. | O.1.d.2.4 | 1900 | I.33.c.15.75 – I.32.d.80.95. |

Approx. 5° of Traverse to left per gun.

4 Guns under Lieut. Crawford will take up position in the "Jumping Off" Trench (Hill Trench) and will accompany the assaulting waves. Their positions will be as follows:

1 Gun on Right Flank

2 Guns on Left Flank.

1 Gun at Junction of Units of 86th Bde.

4 Guns (87th) under Lieut. W.S. Nolan take up positions in Northern end of Hill Trench (about O.2 Central). The particular duty of these guns is Surprise Effect, and fire will be reserved until such time as the enemy opens fire, when he will be engaged, and his fire neutralized.

4 Guns (87th) under Lieut. G.S.J. Downes to be in Hill Trench at Zero minus 1 hour to garrison this trench if the assault is successful.

4 Guns (87th) in strong points D. E. F. G.

13. **Fire**

Artillery. The attack will take place under an intense Artillery Barrage. During the day there will be a slow bombardment of the Enemy's position, special attention being paid to suspected Hostile Machine guns.

**Machine Guns**

At Zero. the Machine Guns of the Division will open a Barrage.

**Stokes Mortars**

At Zero the Stokes Mortars of the 86th Bde will open an intense fire on the hostile trench running from O.2.b.4.5. to the North Edge of the Bois des Aubepines.

The Stokes Mortars of the 37th Division at the same hour have been ordered to open intense fire from the Block in Hook Trench to the road at O.8.B.4.4.

14. **Preliminary Reconnaissance**

As the operation will be carried out under cover of darkness the following points will be attended to:-

(a) Range chart for new situation.
(b) Night firing masks & flash screens.
(d) Luminous sights & limitations of Traverse.
(e) Avenues of approach & defined limits of advance.
(f) Communication
(g) Ammunition, water, oil, Belt filling & repair shelters.
(h) Position of nearest Telephone & Signal station
(i) Liason with Infantry
(j) Location of Headquarters, (Bde, Battr, & Company)
(k) Marginal safety & Depression stops.

15. **Observers**

Observers must keep a sharp look out for the S.O.S. signal, which is a succession of Red Very Lights. On the S.O.S. being sent up, all guns will open at the maximum rate of fire on the barrage line, which will be maintained until our Artillery has well opened, when our Guns will drop to a slower rate of fire.

16. **Dress**

The mobile section will be in fighting order, the N.C.O. taking over a 2 gallon petrol tin of water in his pack. 2 picks and 2 shovels being carried by the teams for the making of emplacements.

17. **Report**

To be sent back as early as possible.

29th May 1917

Edward Dreyfort Major
Comdg 86 Co. Machine Gun Corps

Secret.                                   N° 20 Ope. order

Subject  _Machine Gun Operations_
of _86th Machine Gun Company_
          by Major E. Beckwith. M.C.

Reference
Corps Trench Map 1/10000

1. _Precis of operations 86th Brigade_

The 29th Division attacked 29/30th May 1917 Hook Trench and Tool Trench from O.2.b.4.0. to O.8.b.2.1.

The attack took place at 11.30 p.m. 30th May and was carried out by Two Battalions of the Brigade and one Battalion of the 112th Inf. Brigade.

2. _Preliminary Reconnaissance_

On receipt of Brigade Orders, I made a reconnaissance and defined the plan of operations for my guns

All guns were in their positions 24 hours before the operation and were carefully registered.

The Operation was explained to all Section Officers and a copy of orders was issued to them.

Each Officer made a reconnaissance of his positions and rendered a report that he had made himself acquainted with :-

(a) Avenues of approach (own and enemy's)
(b) System of Communication
(c) Ammunition and Water Dumps.
(d) Belt Filling Shelter, and
(f) made progressive range cards.

### 3. Ammunition Supply

Ammunition Supply was easily maintained owing to previous forward ammunition Dumps having been made.

Each gun had its normal supply of Belt-Boxes — 14: And a further supply of 10,000 rds of S.A.A. was dumped with each gun.

### 4. Water Supply and Spare Parts

Each Non Commissioned Officer of the Mobile Section going over the top carried a 2 gallon tin of water in his pack, and a further supply was carried by each man of the Team in an extra water bottle.

### 5. Gun Disposition

The whole of the Guns of the Company were in action with two added Guns of the 87th Coy. manned by the personnel of the 86th Coy.

The Guns were grouped under their own officers as follows:—

No 1. Section (less 1 Gun) under Lieut Bennett in Snaffle and Twin Trench.

No 2. Section (less 1 Gun) under Lieut J.H. Orpen in Orchard Trench.

No 3. Section under Lieut. Burn, East side of Monchy Village.

No. 4 Section under Lieut Whipp Goode in Shrapnell Trench.

The

The Mobile Section, (1 Gun of No 1 Section, 1 Gun of No 2 Section, 2 Guns of 87th Coy, [86th Coy Personnel]) was under the immediate orders of Lieut H. Crawford.

Each group remained in their battle emplacements and were given definite tasks. Their role being to

(a) prevent enemy movement
(b) assist the Infantry in obtaining superiority of fire
(c) make good the positions won.
(d) pursue the enemy with fire.
(e) cover the reorganisation of the Infantry
(f) repel counter attack
(g) cover retirement in the event of the attack proving unsuccessful.

## Mobile Section

4 Guns were detailed to accompany the Infantry

1 Gun on Right Flank
2 Guns on Left Flank
1 Gun at Junction of Units of 86th Inf Bde

with orders to follow the last wave of the Infantry. The progress of the Infantry to be carefully watched so that the guns could be got forward at the earliest possible moment. Their orders being

(a) To carefully watch the progress of the Infantry so that the guns can be got forward at the earliest possible moment.
(b) To deal with any contingency that may arise during the assault.

4.

(c) to protect the Infantry during Consolidation
(d) In case of Enemy counter attack to assist in driving back enemy forces by rapid production of great fire power at any required point.
(e) occupy Strong Posts prepared by Infantry and assist in holding position gained
(f) to protect the Flank to which they have been allotted

At Zero our Infantry advanced under cover of our Barrage. Two of the Mobile Guns one on the Right & in the Centre were pushed over with the assault & engaged the enemy. The Guns on the left did not go over.

## Attack

The troops of the Assaulting Infantry at about an hour before Zero (2330) began to move out to the taped line, but the Enemy was very much on the alert and threw up a considerable number of "Very Lights" and the movement of our troops was observed. At about 10 minutes before Zero, The Enemy shelled our trenches and searched the ground with Machine Gun Fire.

At Zero our Barrage fell, Artillery and Machine Guns opening with intense fire which was maintained for about 1½ hours

Most of the objective was reached but owing to Hostile Bombing attacks we were unable to maintain the ground won and the situation at dawn was we were holding our original line.

1st June 1917

Edward D. Goforth Major
Comdg 86 Co. Machine Gun Corps

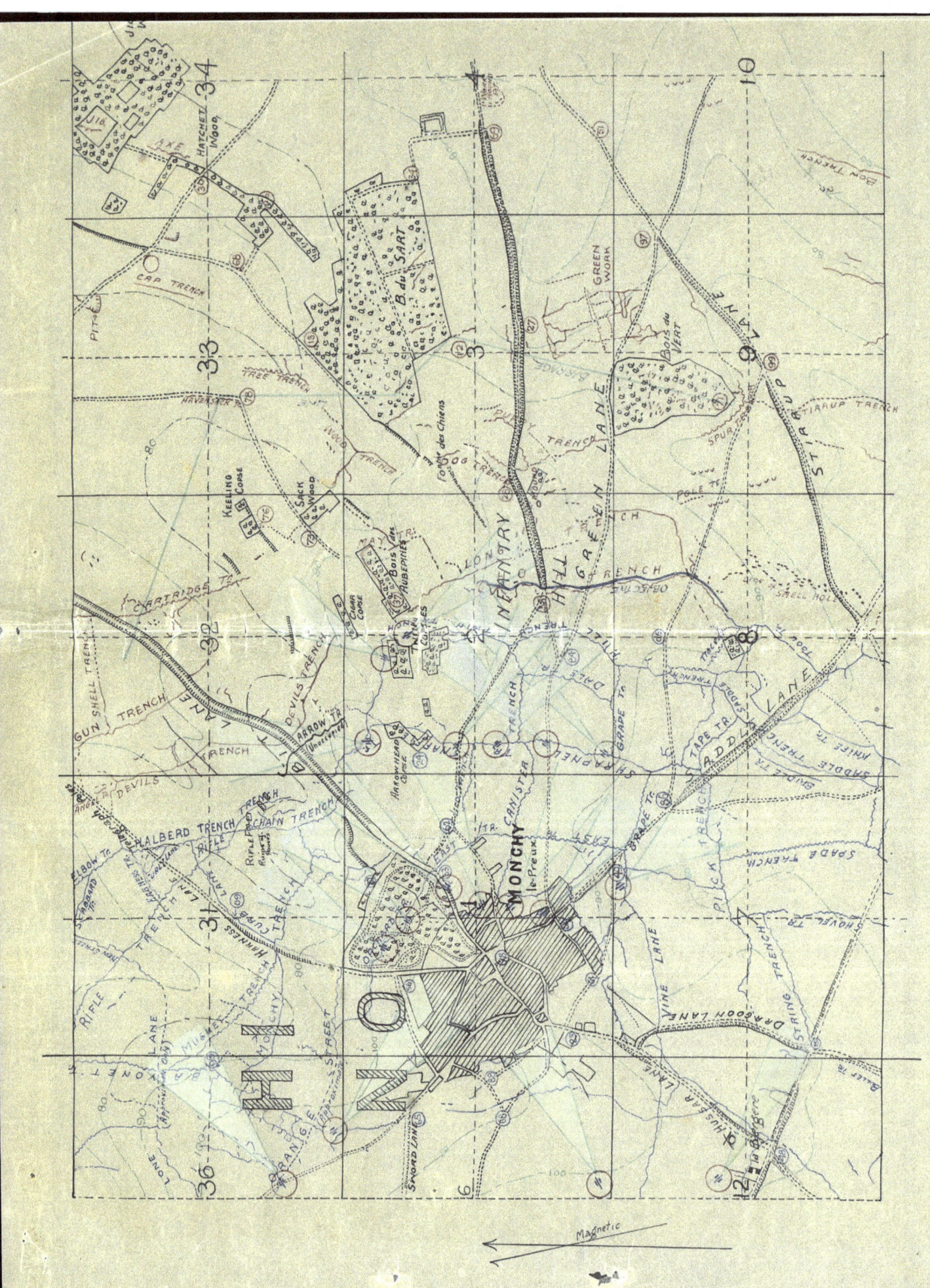

Vol 16

<u>Confidential</u>

<u>War Diary</u>

of the

<u>86th Coy, Machine Gun Corps.</u>

for the period

<u>1st June 1917 to 30th June 1917</u>

<u>Volume XVI</u>

Army Form C. 2118.

# WAR DIARY
## or
## INTELLIGENCE SUMMARY.

Vol XVI

86th Company Machine Gun Corps

Instructions regarding War Diaries and Intelligence Summaries are contained in F. S. Regs., Part II. and the Staff Manual respectively. Title pages will be prepared in manuscript.

| Place | Date | Hour | Summary of Events and Information | Remarks and references to Appendices |
|---|---|---|---|---|
| ARRAS | 1st June 1917 | | The Company rested for the day. Transport was prepared to move at an early hour after midnight. | |
| | 2nd June | | Moved by march route to BERNEVILLE and billeted for the night | |
| BERNEVILLE | 3rd June | | The Company entrained for ST HILIARE from BEAUMETZ Station arrived at CANDAS and marched to Billets at St Hiliare arriving at 5 p.m. Brilliant weather. | |
| ST HILIARE | 4th June to 10th June | | 2 men Jones from Base Drivers Barrell and Bennett 1 Sergeant and 6 ORs returned to Base not likely to become efficient Machine gunners. A class of 1.3.2. ORs attached for Machine Gun Instruction from the Units in the Brigade. Overhauling of kit and general Instruction was carried out daily. The weather was brilliant and the health of the men greatly improved | |

(A7092). Wt. W1859/M1293. 75,000. 1/17. D. D. & L., Ltd. Forms/C.2118/14

Army Form C. 2118.

# WAR DIARY
## or
## INTELLIGENCE SUMMARY.
(Erase heading not required.)

Instructions regarding War Diaries and Intelligence Summaries are contained in F. S. Regs., Part II. and the Staff Manual respectively. Title pages will be prepared in manuscript.

| Place | Date | Hour | Summary of Events and Information | Remarks and references to Appendices |
|---|---|---|---|---|
| ST HILIARE | 16/6/17 | | The Commanding Officer (Major E. BECKWITH) and Lieut. K.M. MOIR proceeded to the U.K. on leave. The Adjutant (Lieut. H.W. ROBINSON) returned from U.K. off leave. 47 Men including 3 Sergeants joined from Base as reinforcements. | |
| | 16- | | 2nd Lieut: A.G. HYAMS joined from the Base for duty with the Company vice 2nd Lieut: Lewis Howse to U.K. wounded. Drill, Route Marches and Musketry was carried out. The Brigade held a sports day. The Company won prizes in the "Boot Race" and "Marching Order Competition". The Division held a "Horse Show". The Company took 1st prize in the "Driving Competition". | |
| | 17th | | The Company moved by march route from ST HILIARE to HALLOY arriving about 12 noon. | |

(A7092). Wt. W12859/M1293. 75,000. 1/17. D. D. & L., Ltd. Forms/C2118/14

# WAR DIARY
## or
## INTELLIGENCE SUMMARY.

*(Erase heading not required.)*

Army Form C. 2118.

| Place | Date | Hour | Summary of Events and Information | Remarks and references to Appendices |
|---|---|---|---|---|
| HALLOY | 1917 18th June | | Drill & small machine Gun Schemes, "Defence of a Village" & "Village" attack | |
| | | | of Village" and firing was carried out. | |
| | 26th June | | The Company moved by march route with Transport & entrained to CANDAS STATION and then entrained for REXPOEDE (MAP. BELGIUM. HAZEBRUCK 5A 1/100.000) detrained and marched to HAANDEKET arriving 5.30 am 27th inst | |
| HAANDEKET | 27th June | | The Company were partly Billeted and part under Canvas. Billet accommodation being limited as most of the surrounding Villages were occupied by recently arrived Fresh Troops. | |
| | 28th June to 30th June | | Drill, Marching Order, Gun Instruction & Route Marching Carried out. Lieut: A. Hosegood and Corporal Priestly returned from CAMIERS having completed a Course of Instruction there. Corporals Murphy and Edwards proceeded to CAMIERS. | |

Army Form C. 2118.

# WAR DIARY
## or
## INTELLIGENCE SUMMARY.

(Erase heading not required.)

| Place | Date | Hour | Summary of Events and Information | Remarks and references to Appendices |
|---|---|---|---|---|
| HAANDEKET | 30th June 1917 | | Continued:— For a Course of Instruction. Lieut. J.H. ORPEN and Sergeant HILLMAN proceeded to U.K. on leave. The latter (Sergt Hillman) for one month having completed his term of service in the Army and elected to remain with the Colours for the duration of the WAR. Strength of Company 30th June 1917. Officers 11. W.O. 1 Sergeants 9 Corporals 9 L.Cpls 5 Men 157 Attached for instruction 51 Total 243 | |

E.S. Beckfort Major
Comdg 80th Company
9. Machine Gun Corps
4th July 1917.

No 17

Confidential

War Diary

of

86th Company. Machine Gun Corps

From 1st July 1917. To 31st July 1917.

Volume XVII

Army Form C. 2118.

# WAR DIARY
## or
## INTELLIGENCE SUMMARY.

86th Company Machine Gun Corps (Erase heading not required.) Vol. XVII.

Instructions regarding War Diaries and Intelligence Summaries are contained in F. S. Regs., Part II. and the Staff Manual respectively. Title pages will be prepared in manuscript.

| Place | Date | Hour | Summary of Events and Information | Remarks and references to Appendices |
|---|---|---|---|---|
| Aardenbek | July 1st | | The Company paraded at 9-15 a.m. for Church Service. Weather:- Very wet. | |
| | 2nd | | The Company paraded at 5-30 a.m. with towels and marched to baths. In the afternoon one hours gas Chest drill was done and at the gas N.C.O. Lieut. Lyle orders received to move to U.K. Weather:- Fine. | |
| | 3rd | | The Company paraded at 8-45 a.m. as pleasing as possible for route march. Weather:- Brilliant Sunshine. Very hot. | |
| | 4th | | The Company paraded at 9 a.m. for drill rifle exercises. At 2 a.m. the backing of limbers was carried out preparatory to moving. Weather:- Dull but fine. | |
| Dragon Camp | 5th | | No. 1 & No. 4 Sections proceeded by march route to DRAGON CAMP. No. 2 Section and transport moved to Camp in PROVEN AREA. Weather:- Very hot. | |
| | 6th | | No. 1 Section relieved one Section of the 86th M.G. Coy. in the A defence area at ELVERDINGHE. No. 4 Section relieved 4 guns of the 86th M.G. Coy. in Anti-aircraft positions. No. 4 Section relieved H. guns of the 86th M.G. Coy in Anti-aircraft positions. Hostile were established in DRAGON CAMP. During the night enemy aeroplanes dropped bombs in the vicinity of the camp at PROVEN. Weather:- Sunny. Hot. | |
| | 7th | | Anti-aircraft guns at HARINGHE WATER WORKS relieved by the 87th M.G. Coy. Repeated gas alarms during night. | |
| | 8, 9, 10, 11 | | General cleaning up of camp carried out. Enemy shelled back area in close proximity to camp. LIEUT. H.V. EVERETT was admitted to hospital on the 9th his place being taken by LIEUT. K.M. MOIR. | |

(A7091). Wt. W12350/M1793. 75,000. 1/17. D. D. & L., Ltd. Forms/C.2118/4

Army Form C. 2118.

# WAR DIARY
## or
## INTELLIGENCE SUMMARY.

(Erase heading not required.) Vol. XVII.

86th Company Machine Gun Corps

| Place | Date | Hour | Summary of Events and Information | Remarks and references to Appendices |
|---|---|---|---|---|
| Dugout Camp. | July 12th | | During the morning the enemy shelled the Camp, the following casualties occurring:— Sgt. Reid F.W. 30941. died of wounds. " Wild R. 20965 wounded Pte. Stewart J. 20964 " " Doubleday E.A. 82131 " " Raby J. 85996 " Boot. Geo. " | Lieut. V.H. Often returned from leave to U.K. |
| In the Line | 13th | | Weather. Fine. No. 1 Section was relieved in the L defences by the 87th Coy and then proceeded to the Front Line to relieve the 88th Coy. No. 4 Section and Hdqtrs. proceeded by March route to the Front line and relieved No. H. 3 & 2 Sections under 2/Lieut. Affleck. No. 4 Section under 2/Lieut. Attkinson was detailed to make the 86th M.G. Coy. the forthcoming emplacements for the barrage emplacements for the forthcoming intensity. The canal bank and pillbox intensity. Weather fine. Warm. | |
| | 14th | | Fairly quiet during day but about 8 p.m. a heavy hostile barrage was put down on the Banal Bank. 2/Lt. J. Floud accidentally wounded by barbed wire. Weather fine. | |
| | 15th | | Very quiet. Major J. Beckwith, commanding officer was wounded in the arm, a fatigue party returning to rear Hdqtrs was caught by enemy fire in BRIELEN. The following casualties resulting:— No. 81250 L/Cpl. D. McBeath. Killed. " 68570 " J.W. J.R. Johnson —do— " 89347 " J.A. Hamming Died of wounds " 89077 " A. Moss —do— " 81248 " J. Kaye Wounded " 81325 " Pte. Billingham —do— " 83057 " G.W. Harrison —do— Weather cool. Following strong wind. | |

Army Form C. 2118.

# WAR DIARY
## or
## INTELLIGENCE SUMMARY.

(Erase heading not required.) Vol. XVII

86th Company Machine Gun Corps.

| Place | Date | Hour | Summary of Events and Information | Remarks and references to Appendices |
|---|---|---|---|---|
| In the Line. | July 1918 | | | |
| | 17.7.18 | | 2nd Lt. Oxer took command of the Company. 2nd Lieut. Wood posted to Company. No. 66945 Sjt. Libby H. wounded. Front with parts was again heavily shelled. No guns cooperated with the artillery firing 2000 rds per gun per night on specially selected targets. Very quiet work on barrage emplacements & improved wiring during Wiring was put in hand again, cooperated with Artillery. | |
| | 19th | | Very quiet day. The 1st Bttn (K.O.S.B.) made a raid on the enemy trenches during the night. The machine guns assisted with a barrage on the flanks of our troops. Nr. 67977 Rifleman H.J. wounded. | |
| | | | Capt. J.S. Roberts posted to command the Company. Brilliant Sunshine. Weather. | |
| | 20th | | The Company was relieved in the line by the 113th & 114th Companies and marched to Corps Staging Area No. 2. Weather very hot. | |
| | 21st | | The Company cleaned equipment, guns, tripods etc. and re bucked kirbies. The men were noted as much as possible. Weather. very hot. | |
| | 22nd | | The Company paraded at 9.40 am for Church Services. Tents in vicinity of the camp. During the night, hostile aircraft dropped bombs but did not reach. Weather very hot. | |
| | 23rd | | The Company paraded at 9am and carried out Drill rifle exercises. The guns, tripods & equipment were cleaned. Weather very hot. | |

Army Form C. 2118.

# WAR DIARY
## or
## INTELLIGENCE SUMMARY.

(Erase heading not required.) Vol. XVII.

No. 2 Company Machine Gun Corps.

| Place | Date | Hour | Summary of Events and Information | Remarks and references to Appendices |
|---|---|---|---|---|
| Corps Staging Camp and 7/8.2. | July 24th | | The Company paraded at 11.55 a.m. and proceeded by march route to PROVEN No. 3. Area. and were billeted in camp. | |
| | 25th | | No.1. Section proceeded to HARINGHE Water Works and relieved one section of No 88th M.G. Coy. on A.A. defence duty. Weather. Very hot. | |
| | 26th | | No. 3 & 4 Sections paraded at 6 a.m. and marched to Brigade rendezvous to take part in Field day. No. 2 Section paraded in loose dress with towels at 9 a.m. for bathing. Weather very very warm. The Company practised loading from limbers to pack. An attack was practised in the afternoon. Very hot. Weather. Very hot. | |
| | 27th | | The Company practised laying guns for Barrage work in the morning. The remainder of No. 1 Section relieved the first party at HARINGHE Water Works. Weather fine & warm. | |
| | 28. | | Church parade as usual. Weather rain throughout the day. | |
| | 29th | | The Company practised (a) the selection & occupation of positions (b) Laying guns for + overhead } fire 2 indirect } fire (3) advancing machine guns in attack Weather. dull | |

Army Form C. 2118.

# WAR DIARY
## or
## INTELLIGENCE SUMMARY.

(Erase heading not required.) Vol. XVII.

86th Company Machine Gun Corps.

| Place | Date | Hour | Summary of Events and Information | Remarks and references to Appendices |
|---|---|---|---|---|
| Corps Staging Area No. 2 | July 30th | | No Coy. less part of No. 1 Section (aircraft duty) paraded at 11-15 a.m. and proceeded by March Route to Proven No. 2 Area. | |
| " | 31st | | The Coy. paraded at 9 a.m. for unpacking limbers & cleaning guns. Weather:- Very wet. | |

Confidential

War Diary

of the

86th Company - Machine Gun Corps

for the month

from 1st August 1917 to 31st August 1917.

Volume 18.

Vol 18

Army Form C. 2118.

# WAR DIARY
## or
## INTELLIGENCE SUMMARY.
(Erase heading not required.)

86th Machine Gun Corps  Vol. XVIII

Instructions regarding War Diaries and Intelligence Summaries are contained in F.S. Regs., Part II. and the Staff Manual respectively. Title pages will be prepared in manuscript.

| Place | Date | Hour | Summary of Events and Information | Remarks and references to Appendices |
|---|---|---|---|---|
| Info. Depot No. 2. | Aug 1st | | The Company paraded at 9 a.m. Rain prevented any outdoor work being done. Officers cleaning the Camp. | |
| | 2nd | | The Company paraded for ½ at 9 a.m. for lecture on Selection Occupation of Positions. L/Cpls B/s were instructed in Gun Laying for Indirect fire. Remainder of morning being taken up with cleaning guns. Wet. Very wet. | |
| | 3rd | | No outdoor training was possible owing to continued rain. Lecture by C.O. to Officers on German Raids during afternoon. Retreat precautions against gas. | |
| | 4th | | The Company paraded at 9 a.m. for Gun cleaning. Weather very wet. | |
| | 5th | | The Company paraded at 11.45 p.m. and marched out to Maple Copse into the forward area arriving about 8 p.m. No. 84561 Pte Price wounded by bomb from hostile aeroplane. | |
| | 6th | | The Company paraded for inspection at 11 a.m. spent remainder of the day cleaning. 3/Lieut J.W. Goode wounded. Weather. Fine afternoon stormy. | |
| No. 16. camp. | 7th | | The Company paraded at 9 a.m. for cleaning, maintaining guns, 1st relief of No 1, 2 & 3 sections paraded at 3.30 p.m. marched to the line to relieve the Guards Coy in the BOESINGHE SECTOR. The remainder of Coy with transport marched into Camp Herzele Torre Area. | |
| Herzeele Torre Area. | 8th | | In the Line. Reliefs were arranged for Nos 1, 2 & 3 sections. No. 64702 Pte C. Burton, No. 39877 Pte Wain wounded. | |

# WAR DIARY
## or
## INTELLIGENCE SUMMARY.

Army Form C. 2118.

(Erase heading not required.) *No. XVIII*

161st Brigade Machine Gun Corps.

| Place | Date | Hour | Summary of Events and Information | Remarks and references to Appendices |
|---|---|---|---|---|
| In the Line | 9th | | The remainder of Company in tents handed over to Lewis making Headles line return. | |
| | 10th | | Less reactioned reliefs took place in the line. Weather fine warm. | |
| | | | During this month the following casualties occurred:— wounded | |
| | | | No. 60191 L/Cpl Toth H. | |
| | | | No. 21008 Pte. Doyle | |
| | | | 71015 " Hoyt | |
| | | | 71943 L/Cpl McAuley | |
| | | | 81675 Pte Harris  } missing | |
| | | | 14009 " Hagley | |
| | | | 10769 " Jones | |
| | | | 86585 " Forth | |
| | | | " Wallace | |
| | 11th | | In the Line. | |
| | 12th | | Nos 2 & 3 Sections were relieved in the Line by the 229th Coy. No. 1 Section remaining in. | |
| | 13th | | The Company noted preparing to going into the attack. Weather dull & showery. | |
| | 14th | | The Company went into the Line two Sections took up barrage positions No. 3099th the remaining Section by the whistlings arm a. wounded. | |
| | 15th | | Heavy Bombardment by our artillery. Weather very wet. | |
| | 16th | | The Company co-operated in the operations carried out by the 29th Divn. the attack took place at 4-45 am. Observation. Guns co attached. | |

# WAR DIARY or INTELLIGENCE SUMMARY

Army Form C. 2118.

Vol. XVIII

| Place | Date | Hour | Summary of Events and Information | Remarks and references to Appendices |
|---|---|---|---|---|
| In the Line | Aug. 16th (a.m.) | | The following casualties occurred:— No. 71931 Pte. McEvoy, " 295177 " Dyke, " 84193 " Foscitt, " 84854 " Hopkins. Weather:- Brilliant sunshine. | |
| | 23rd | | Reliefs were carried out among H.S. Teams. The guns were employed on barrage work and harassing fire and maintained throughout each night. Particular attention was paid to the right flank owing to the enemy concentrating in that direction. | |
| | 24th | | Shelter was arranged. The shelter was viewed in the line by the No. 329th Coy. and were billeted in the camp to the front area. A coys of 3 signallers was posted to the Coy. Weather:- Rainy. | |
| Forest Area | 25th | | The Company rested in the morning. In the afternoon the men cleaned their equipment etc. Weather:- Rainy. | |
| | 26th | | The Company started trekking at 9 hours and moved by march route to POINT CAMP arriving about 2.30 hrs. Heavy rain during night. Weather:- Dull. | |
| Point Camp | 27th | | The Company bivouacs for the inspection at 9 am. Lectures were re-organised and equipment was cleaned. Weather:- Showery. | |

Army Form C. 2118.

# WAR DIARY
## or
## INTELLIGENCE SUMMARY.
(Erase heading not required.) Vol XVIII

Instructions regarding War Diaries and Intelligence Summaries are contained in F. S. Regs., Part II. and the Staff Manual respectively. Title pages will be prepared in manuscript. 4th Coy. Army Machine Gun Corps.

| Place | Date | Hour | Summary of Events and Information | Remarks and references to Appendices |
|---|---|---|---|---|
| Grit Camp | Aug. 28th | | The Company paraded at 6.45 a.m. and carried out programme of work. Saluting & arms drill. Gun Drill. Stoppages. Clothing. Weather: Cloudy in morning, Fine afternoon. | |
| | 29th | | The Company paraded at 6.30 a.m. and carried out programme of work and drill. Kilating. I.O.E.D. Stoppages. Belt filling, army, training. Instruction of Lange Bodo. Weather: Showery. | |
| | 30th | | The Company paraded at 8.30 a.m. and carried out a programme of work. Company Drill. I.O.E.D. Stoppages. Drill with Light Infantry. | |
| | 31st | | Weather: Showery. | |

OPERATION ORDERS BY CAPTAIN J.P. ROBERTS
COMMANDING 86th COMPANY MACHINE GUN CORPS.

1. The 86th Machine Gun Company will co-operate in the forthcoming operation to be carried out by 29th Division at a date & time to be notified later.

2. The Guns will be disposed of as follows:-
   8 guns (No 1 & No 3 Section) Barrage.
   8 guns (No 2 & No 4 Section) Consolidation.

3. (LOCATION AT ZERO)
   a. **Barrage Guns**: The 4 guns of No 1 Section will form E. group at U.26.a.9.1 and will come under the command of the O.C. 87 M.G.C. on Y/Z night.

   The 4 guns of No 3 Section will form K. group at U.26.d.2.7 and will come under the command of the O.C. 88th M.G.C. on Y/Z night.

   K. group will become DIVISIONAL RESERVE at Z + 1.40 at U.26.c.9.2.

   b. **Consolidating Guns**: Present defensive position

4. TARGETS. Officers in charge of barrage groups will be personally responsible for the correct laying of guns and that D.M.G.O's instructions as issued in APPENDIX A are complied with.

5. GUNS FOR CONSOLIDATING. The 4 guns of No 4 Section will be allotted to the right attacking Brigade (88th Brigade) - 2 guns for each Battalion.
   The 4 guns of No 2 Section will be allotted to the left attacking Brigade (87th Brigade)
   The first Objective will be :- DENNAIN Fm - MARTIN'S MILL to Railway
   Boundaries of attacking Brigades will be :-
   Right Brigade - Rt Boundary - Railway running through U.27.b - U.22.a - U.22.c - U.22.b -
   Left boundary - DENNAIN Fm - U.21.c.2.2 - DENNAIN Fm - U.21.b.4.1
   CAIRNES Fm U.22.a.2.7 - POINT 97 & road to BROMBEEK at U.16.d.1.8
   Left Brigade Left Boundary - line through COLONELS Fm - U.20.c.2.2 - U.25 Central
   U.20.b.9.9 - U.20.b.4.4 - U.15 Central

6. ROLE: These guns will remain in their present defensive position until a time to be notified later. They will then move forward and occupy defensive in the first OBJECTIVE. Section Officers will report to O.C. Battalion commanding his respective sector in their objectives.
   The guns will move forward direct from defensive position.

7. AMMUNITION:- 6 boxes per gun. In addition to which all ranks will carry two bandoliers.

8. RATIONS:- 2 days ration, in addition to iron rations, will be carried on each man. Full waterbottles to be carried.

9. DUMPS:- Officers doing barrage will be responsible for the construction of forward dumps of S.A.A. and water. These will be completed by X/Y night.
For guns going forward S.A.A. and water dumps will be formed at SIGNAL FARM.

10. DRESS:- Fighting Order. All ranks will be dressed alike and will carry one bomb and two sandbags.

11. COMMUNICATION:- (a) One Orderly per section will report at WOOD HOUSE for guns doing barrage.
    (2) One runner per team will report to Advanced H.Q. - SIGNAL FARM from guns going forward after they are in position.
    (3) A cycle orderly will be at BOESINGHE CHATEAU & will keep touch with rear H.Q.
    (4) Guns going forward will use location screens.
    (5) Full use will be made of Battalion signalling arrangements

12. MEDICAL ARRANGEMENTS:- Machine Gunners will make use of Battalion arrangements with whom they are co-operating.

13. CHQ. WOOD HOUSE C.2.a.2.8. Advanced HQ. SIGNAL FARM.

Issue copies to:-
1. D.M.C.O.
2. Office
3. 29th M.C.C.
4. 88th "
5. 86th Brigade
6. 87th "
7. 88th "
8-11 Section Officers
12 War Diary

APPENDIX II

## 29th DIVISION M.G. BARRAGE INSTRUCTIONS.

1. **GUNS AVAILABLE:** 227th M.G.C. — 16 guns
   86 — (less 2 Sections) — 8
   87 — 8
   88 — 8
   **TOTAL 40 guns.**

2. **DISTRIBUTION:** These guns will be divided into 10 groups of 4 guns each (A-K). For purposes of preparation and control these will be divided into 3 large groups as follows:-
   1 Group. A. B. C. D. found by 227th M.G.C. under OC 227th M.G.C.
   2   "   { E. F. G. }    87th   " } OC 87 M.G.C.
   3   "   { H. I. J. K. } 88th   " } OC 88th M.G.C.

   These groups will be along the general line LOEBECK FARM – MATOS FARM – ABRI F – U.26 Central – U.26.d.8.6 with A group at LOEBECK FARM and K group at U.26.d.8.6

3. **EMPLACEMENTS:** Pits may be dug or shell holes converted. In either case the platform must be sandbagged & made firm. Tripods must be bedded in sandbags to prevent sinking. 32 Circular tables are available if required. The lower limit of Traverse must be blocked. Aiming posts giving off limits of traverse & search will be put up for each gun before Y day.

4. **AMMUNITION:** 32 belts per gun will be the average amount fired. Each barrage gun will be provided with 8 spare belts in addition to the existing 32 belts per gun. These will be filled before Zero. 400,000 rounds S.A.A. is being gone up to ABRI WOOD and from this dumps of 40,000 rounds will be made by each group of 4 guns.

5. **RATE OF FIRE:** One belt in 5 minutes during an advance & 1 belt in 10 minutes during a pause. Belt filling arrangements must be made to keep up with this rate as far as possible.

6. **WATER:** One petrol tin per gun and 1 tin per gun team to be at each gun position before Zero.

7. **BARRELS:** Each gun will start with a new barrel. A few rounds should be fired beforehand to remove grease sticking. Barrels will be changed on completion of barrage. Not more than one gun per group to change barrels at a time.

8. **BEARINGS:** All compasses should be tested and cross used. Steel between and tripods should not be near enough to affect bearings. As there are few landmarks each group should erect posts at suitable distances for reference objects. Gun positions must be checked by measurement as well as by Section. Range finding instruments can be used for this.

9. **DANGER SPACE.** Each group commander will arrange to mark out the danger space immediately in front of his group and will arrange to warn troops in the neighbourhood. The danger space must not include any regular track or duck walk that will be required for communication or reinforcements.

Vol 19

# Confidential

## War Diary

of the

### 86th Company. Machine Gun Corps.

for the period

From 1st September 1917 to 30th September 1917.

Volume XIX

Army Form C. 2118.

# WAR DIARY
or
# INTELLIGENCE SUMMARY.

(Erase heading not required.)

Instructions regarding War Diaries and Intelligence Summaries are contained in F.S. Regs., Part II. and the Staff Manual respectively. Title pages will be prepared in manuscript.

Company Machine Gun Corps. No. XIX

| Place | Date | Hour | Summary of Events and Information | Remarks and references to Appendices |
|---|---|---|---|---|
| POINT CAMP | SEPT. 1st | | | |
| " | 2nd | | The Company paraded at 8.30 a.m. and carried out programme of work including Company Drill, T.O.E.T. use of ground of cover. 2/Lieut. A.H. Hopgood proceeded on leave to U.K. The Company paraded for Church Service. The G.O.C. inspected the transport and expressed his satisfaction. Weather:- Dull windy. | |
| " | 3rd | | The Company paraded at 8.30 a.m. & carried out programme of work. Enemy Aeroplanes very active, dropping bombs in vicinity of camp. They were fired on by A.A. guns & wounded in the camp. Full moon at night. Weather:- fine. | |
| " | 4th | | The Company paraded at 8.30 a.m. and Swedish Remedial Drill. 2/Lieut. V.W. Smith reported for duty. | |
| " | 5th | | The Company paraded at 8.30 a.m. and carried out programme of work for the day. 2/Lieut. A.G. Hyams struck off strength of Coy. Nominal roll for G.O.C.'s inspection on 17th instant. Results RFs 3 M.G.Coy O. The Coy. played 2nd Royal Fus. on 17th instant. Single Machine. Enemy aeroplanes very active during night. Weather:- Single Machine. | |
| " | 6th | | The Company paraded at 8.30 a.m. and carried out programme parade. Weather:- very hot day. | |
| " | 7th | | The Company paraded at 8.30 a.m. and carried out programme of work. A party of 25 visited the seaside motor lorries being used to convey the party. Weather:- fine warm. | |

Army Form C. 2118.

# WAR DIARY
## or
## INTELLIGENCE SUMMARY.

(Erase heading not required.) Vol. XIX

Instructions regarding War Diaries and Intelligence Summaries are contained in F. S. Regs., Part II. and the Staff Manual respectively. Title pages will be prepared in manuscript. 86th Company Machine Gun Corps.

| Place | Date | Hour | Summary of Events and Information | Remarks and references to Appendices |
|---|---|---|---|---|
| POINT CAMP. | 1917 8th | | | |
| | 9th | | The Company paraded at 8.30 and carried out arms and saluting, action from flanks, sections in attack. Weather:- Bright Sunshine. | |
| | 10th | | Church Parade at 9 am & 9.45 am. The Company paraded at 8.15 am and carried out Barrage fire. Kit Inspection under Section arrangements. Weather:- Bright Sunshine. The Company paraded at 8.15 am and carried out Barrage fire. 2/Lieut. G.H. Baird gave lecture to Officers 17.15.0 on Barrage fire. Weather:- Bright Sunshine. | |
| | 11th | | The Company paraded at 8.15 am and carried out Barrage fire. No. 20939 Pte. Mc Carthy of this Company joined the Brigade Sports took place. Very hot. in the afternoon the long jump. Weather:- Bright Sunshine. | |
| | 12th | | The Company paraded at 8.15 am and carried out Company Drill. Gun drill on the Reparators Elevation Rotation of Ontario. A lecture was given by O.C. 15th Wing R.F.C. 2/Lieut. A.H. Hogart returned from leave to U.K. | |
| | 13th, 14th, 15th | | The Company paraded at 8.15 am and carried out Company Drill, Barrage Drill. Elevens Rotation Drill with Limbers. Company Transport was cleaned. The Limbers were frequently Inspected to all guns & equipment was clean. No. 11693 Sgt. A.E. Millman promoted W.O. class II appointed Co. M. 87th Coy. | |
| | 16th | | The Company paraded at 7.15 am marched down at 9.45 am. The Company paraded about 6 pm Marched route to camp at HERZEELE arriving about 6 pm by march route. Transport remained at POINT CAMP. (Details of H.Q.'s) Weather:- Very hot. | |

Army Form C. 2118.

# WAR DIARY
## or
## INTELLIGENCE SUMMARY.

(Erase heading not required.) Vol. XIX

Instructions regarding War Diaries and Intelligence Summaries are contained in F. S. Regs., Part II. and the Staff Manual respectively. Title pages will be prepared in manuscript. 86: Machine Gun Company.

| Place | Date | Hour | Summary of Events and Information | Remarks and references to Appendices |
|---|---|---|---|---|
| HERZEELE | 17th 18th 19th | | The Company competed with the Battalions of the 86th Brigade in Brigade Sports. The afternoon of the 19th the Company paraded and marched by road & route to Point Camp arriving about 5.30 p.m. Weather: Bright | |
| POINT CAMP. | 20th | | The Limbers were packed and proceeded by road to Leo in FOREST AREA. The Company paraded and marched to ROVEN where they entrained and proceeded to WELLINGTON CAMP, arriving about 4 p.m. The camp was pitched during the evening. Weather: Dull. | |
| WELLINGTON CAMP (L. reserve) | 21st | | The Company paraded at 8.45 a.m. and worked on improvement of camp. Enemy aeroplanes were very active during afternoon. Drinking tanks being supplied in vicinity of camp. Weather: very bright. | |
| " | 22nd to 25th | | The Company furnished a working party consisting of two sections for work on roads. A range was made in the vicinity of the camp and firing practices were carried out. Enemy aeroplanes were very active at night. Weather: Very bright generally. | |
| " | 26th | | A working party of one section repaired roads. Remainder of Company carried out a tactical scheme. | |
| " | 27th | | The Company paraded at 9 a.m. and carried out a programme of work. They twice practiced on musketry practice. The No.4 Section relieved a section of the 217th Coy in the line. Enemy aeroplanes very active with bombs during the night. Weather: Very bright. | |

Army Form C. 2118.

# WAR DIARY
## or
## INTELLIGENCE SUMMARY.
(Erase heading not required.) Vol XIX

86th Company Machine Gun Corps.

Instructions regarding War Diaries and Intelligence Summaries are contained in F. S. Regs., Part II. and the Staff Manual respectively. Title pages will be prepared in manuscript.

| Place | Date Sept. | Hour | Summary of Events and Information | Remarks and references to Appendices |
|---|---|---|---|---|
| WELLINGTON CAMP | 28th | | | |
| | 29th | | The Company paraded at 8.45 am for Squad Drill Saluting, Consolidation of Rifle Exercises, Barrage Drill. Enemy aeroplanes very active. Weather:- Very warm. Bright moon. | |
| " | 30th | | Church Parade at 10.20 am & 11.30 am. Enemy aeroplanes very active. Weather:- Very warm. Bright moon. | |

**Confidential**

War Diary

of the

86th Company - Machine Gun Corps.

for the period

From 1st October 1917 to 31st October 1917.

Volume XX.

Army Form C. 2118.

# WAR DIARY
## or
## INTELLIGENCE SUMMARY.

(Erase heading not required.) Vol XX

86th Company Machine Gun Corps.

Instructions regarding War Diaries and Intelligence Summaries are contained in F. S. Regs., Part II. and the Staff Manual respectively. Title pages will be prepared in manuscript.

| Place | Date Oct. | Hour | Summary of Events and Information | Remarks and references to Appendices |
|---|---|---|---|---|
| WELLINGTON CAMP | 1st | | No. 3 Section in the line. Church Parades for Sections out of line. Enemy aircraft very active. Weather:- Very bright. | |
| " | 2nd 3rd | | The Company paraded at 9 am and carried out Programme of work. The following casualties occurred in the line:- No. 87669 Pte Johnson J. wounded. Pte H. Crawford wounded. No. 83858 Pte Hansen H. -do- | |
| " | 4. | | No.3 Section took part in an attack made by the 29th Division. No. 2 Section took up Barrage positions. Operation Order No. 6 attached. The following casualties occurred:- Lieut J@e Wood wounded. No. 83836 Pte Stapleton J. wounded " 72836 " Oxley A. -do- " 67335 " Nurse D. Killed. Weather:- Stormy. | |
| " | 5. | | The Company were relieved in the line and returned to camp. No. 1. Section paraded for work on new stables. Weather:- Stormy. | |
| " | 6. | | The Company moved from WELLINGTON CAMP to DULWICH CAMP. Weather:- Stormy. | |
| DULWICH CAMP | 7. | | The Company paraded at 11 am. for Gun cleaning etc. 2/Lt. J.H. Olivier posted to the Company. Weather:- Very wet. | |
| " | 8. | | The Company paraded 10 am. and overhauled Guns & equipment preparatory to an attack. The Coy. moved into the line during the evening. Very heavy rain. | |

Army Form C. 2118.

# WAR DIARY
## or
## INTELLIGENCE SUMMARY.

(Erase heading not required.) Vol XX.

86th Inf. Bde. Machine Gun Corps.

Instructions regarding War Diaries and Intelligence Summaries are contained in F. S. Regs., Part II. and the Staff Manual respectively. Title pages will be prepared in manuscript.

| Place | Date Oct. | Hour | Summary of Events and Information | Remarks and references to Appendices |
|---|---|---|---|---|
| Elverdinche | 9th | 9 A. | Rear Headquarters moved into huts at ELVERDINCHE. The Coy. took part in an attack made by the 86th Brigade. The following casualties occurred :— 2/Lieut. J.H. Burd wounded. 2/Lt. S.H. Osborn wounded. Spr. England 2/Lt. P.W. Limb do— Pte. Britten R. Killed. " Hirst E. do — " Marsh J. do — " Coleman J. wounded " Main R.C. do — " Norrish S. do — " Wilson E. do — " Carlon J. do — No. 88024 Cpl. Knightly A. to U.K. for commission. Weather :— Very wet. | |
| " | 10th | | Headquarters 10% Coys moved to PARANA CAMP in PROVEN AREA. The Company were relieved in line during the night 10/11 th. | |
| PROVEN | 11th | | The remainder of Company moved by tram to PROVEN AREA into PARANA CAMP. Transport moved by road. | |
| " | 12 th | | The Company paraded at 10 a.m. for the organisation of Sections. 2/Lieut. J.A. Herrit } Posted to this Coy. 2/Lieut. J.A. Daubly } Weather :— very wet. | |
| | 13th<br>14th<br>15th | | The Coy. paraded at 9.30 a.m. and carried out programme of work. The guns & rifles were cleaned. Weather :— Showery. | |

Army Form C. 2118.

# WAR DIARY
## or
## INTELLIGENCE SUMMARY.
(Erase heading not required.) Vol XX.

86th Coy Machine Gun Corps.

| Place | Date Oct. | Hour | Summary of Events and Information | Remarks and references to Appendices |
|---|---|---|---|---|
| PARANA CAMP | 16th 17th | | The Company paraded at 6.45 a.m. and proceeded by march route to HOPOUTRE SIDING, POPERINGHE where they entrained for BEAUMETZ. Reached BEAUMETZ about 11.30 p.m. after unloading proceeded by march route to BLAIRVILLE arriving about 4 a.m. on the 17th. The remainder of the day was spent in cleaning up. Weather:- Fine. | |
| BLAIRVILLE | 18th 19th | | The Company paraded at 8.30 a.m. and carried out programme of work. Lieut. H.W. Robinson appointed Second in command of Coy. vice Lt. J.A. Orpin wounded. Weather:- Fine frosty. | |
| " | 20th | | Church Parades. | |
| " | 21st to 25th | | The Coy. paraded at 8.30 each morning and carried out programme of work as laid down. 2/Lieut. J.L. Boucke posted to Coy. 22/10/17. Weather:- Fine generally. | |
| " | 26th 27th | | The Company paraded and practised Ceremonial Parades with Brigade. Weather:- etc. | |
| " | 28th | | Church Parades. The following decorations were awarded:- No. 20904 Sgt. W. Walden Bar to M.M. " 30/519 Pot. E. Town Mil. Medal " 812416 Acting S. H. Lowd -do- " 840038 " W. Taylor -do- " 71959 Pte. J.E. Starns -do- | |
| " | 29th 30th | | The Company paraded and carried out programme of work as laid down. 2/Lt. J. Bennett proceeded on leave to U.K. No. 35292 Pte. R.W. Baker No. 97877 Pte. T. Hamel No. 83738 Pte. Jas. Walker posted to Coy. | |
| " | 31st | | The Company paraded & practised Ceremonial Parades with Brigade. | |

13. BARRAGE TABLE (cont):-

Ammunition:- Each gun will commence the barrage with 20 belts filled and 10,000 rounds of S.A.A.

RATES OF FIRE:- 
Z — Z + 20 minutes     1 belt in 4 minutes
Z + 20 — Z + 1 hour    1  "  " 10  "
Z + 1 — Z + 3 "        1  "  " 15  "
Remainder of the day   Intermittent fire
S.O.S.                 1 belt in 1 minute for 4 minutes then 1 belt in 10 minutes.

WATER:- One petrol tin must be at each gun position before Zero.

BARRELS:- Each gun will commence the barrage with a new barrel. These will be changed on completion of the barrage.

COMMUNICATION:- One orderly will report to Company H.Q. on Y/Z night.

7/10/17

N. Robinson Lieut & Adj
184th Company, Machine Gun Corps

Copies to:-
1. Office
2-3. War Diary
4. 61st Brigade
5. 182nd
6. O.M.G.O.
7-10 Section Officers.
11. O.C. 1st R. Dublin Fusiliers

## 96th Machine Gun Company
### Operation Order No. 7

Reference Map. BROEMBEEK

1. In conjunction with Operations to be carried out by the 8th Infantry Brigade at a date and hour to be notified later. The 96th Machine Gun Company will co-operate as detailed under.

2. **Distribution**
   A. Barrage Guns — 8 guns
   B. Reserve Guns — 2 "
   C. Consolidation Guns — 6 "
        2 — Royal Fusiliers
        2 — Berkshire "
        2 — Flank Detachment

3. **Location of Zero**
   A. Guns — U.23.c.4.5
   B. Guns — U.18.c.4.3
   C. Guns — 2 Guns Royal Fusiliers behind first wave of attacking Coys.
        2 Guns Berkshire Fusiliers behind first wave of attacking Coy.
        2 Guns with Flank Detachment behind last platoon of Royal Fusiliers.

   Officer in charge will report to O.C. Battalion concerned when guns are in position. Time guns will be in position will be notified later.

4. **Role**
   A. Guns — are detailed for ultimate barrage fire.
   B. Guns — will remain in present company positions.
   From the 8th minute after zero hour, on orders of the Officer in charge, will report to the C.O. Battalion advancing. Should Battalion Hdrs. two guns will move forward under cover and assist in the consolidation of their objective.

   C. Guns — will move forward under orders of Battalion at such distance as —
        On reaching their objective, they will
        a. Endeavour to form a rallying point for stragglers etc.
        one at a time —

Continued page 2

4. ROLE

(a) Guns shall immediately be called upon to exploit their success. Such as have not allotted to objective Battalions will move forward and consolidate the new objectives i.e. the Purple, Green and Purple lines.

(b) Guns moving with forward Battalions will move in rear of the Royal Fusiliers detachment to Green line objective. They will then move behind detachment of ...... line Battalion as soon as ordered. These guns are responsible for the protection of the right flank. They will fall back pay to stay and on ....... packs of ammunition.

(c) Special protection against ....... ........ Barre Duval and Point ...... Line. The guns forming flank detachment will move forward on the right flank of assaulting Battalion.

5. AMMUNITION

1. Guns going forward will carry at least 6 Belt Boxes in addition to which all ranks will carry bandoliers.

2. A Reserve Dump will be established at U.23 c. .. 3.

3. Should any captured German M.G. Ammunition be found this will be used.

6. COMMUNICATION

Advanced Coy H.Q. will be at U.23 b. 2. 3. with Batt. H.Q. and will move forward with Batt. H.Q.

All messages from forward ...... will be sent to advanced H.Q. and then by runners to ....... H.Q.

Company will make full use of Batt. and Brigade runners and Lepetting arrangements.

C.H.Q. will be at U.23 c. .. 1. It will move to advanced H.Q. as soon as Batt. H.Q. has moved forward.

Location in rear will be carried by Coms going forward. Co is ....... as soon as ....... information will get in touch with the nearest Infantry Coy H.Q.

7. DRESS

Fighting Order. All ranks will be dressed alike.

8. EQUIPMENT

Ranks will march as lightly as possible. 4 bandoliers will be carried by all ranks, 2 of which will be carried over the ....... Guns will be wrapped in ground sheet (to cleaning rod on ....... hurdle) before moving into assembly position.

9. RATIONS

2 days rations and ........
1 tin sandyfies biscuit (if wanted)

10. ZERO

Will be notified later.

Continued page 3

11. WATCHES.    Will be synchronized at Bde. Hd Qrs. [illegible] at
                [illegible]

12. MEDICAL
    ARRANGEMENTS
                [illegible] Bearers will [illegible] positions [illegible] of
                Battalions with whom they are acting.

                                                    J.P. Roberts. Captain

Copies issued to

                        56th Brigade
                        D.A.Q.O.
                        1st Lancashire Fus.
                        2nd Royal      "
                        1st Middlesex Regt.
                        Liaison Officer
                        Diary
                        Office

## A. Barrage Instructions

**No. of Guns:** 4.

**LOCATION:**
1. At ZERO — U.23.a.6.3.
2. After moving forward — U.18.a.

### Barrage Table

Guns during barrage will fire in accordance to table.

| LOCATION | TARGET | Rate of Fire |
|---|---|---|
| U.23.a.6.3 | U.12.a.7.5 — U.7a.2.0 | 1 Belt in 10 mins |
|  | T.18.b.  — U.7a.1.8 | 1 " " 10 " |
|  | U.26.a.3.1 — U.7a.7.9 | 1 " " 10 " |

All guns will be in position ready to fire one hour before ZERO.

Officer in charge will be personally [responsible] for the correct laying of guns.

Each gun will have a barrage chart.

**AMMUNITION:** 10 belt boxes per gun.
10,000 rds. S.A.A.

**WATER:** 1 Petrol can at each position.

**SPARES:** Each gun will about will take [?]

**MOUNTINGS:** Guns will be fired from T shape mountings. These will be taken forward when guns move.

**COMMUNICATIONS:** Orderly will report at Coy. HQ on Z/2.
1 Orderly will report at ONE on night Y/Z. One orderly will be sent down to C.H.Q. from Barrage Position.

**DRESS:** As detailed in B.

J. Roberts, Captain.
Commanding the Company Machine Gun Corps.

Army Form C. 2118.

# WAR DIARY
## or
## INTELLIGENCE SUMMARY

(Erase heading not required.)

86th Bde. M.G. Coy.
November 1917.

Instructions regarding War Diaries and Intelligence Summaries are contained in F.S. Regs., Part II. and the Staff Manual respectively. Title Pages will be prepared in manuscript.

| Place | Date | Hour | Summary of Events and Information | Remarks and references to Appendices |
|---|---|---|---|---|
| ETAPLES Camp No.2 | 1/11/17 | | Training. Strong 1 O.R. from hospital. 3 O.R. from Rest Camp. | |
| " | 2/11/17 | | Training. Brigade Practice Ceremonial Parade for presentation of Military Medal ribbons to O.I.M.C. Captain H.J.DE. L.M.M. Pts Virgo and Cpl Allen. Weather fair | |
| " | 3/11/17 | 1500 | Training. 1 O.R. to hospital. Weather fair. | |
| " | 4/11/17 | | Weather fair | |
| " | 5/11/17 | 1430 | Training. Cross Country Competition. Weather poor. | |
| " | 6/11/17 | | Training. 1 O.R. to strength of Battery. 1 O.R. returned to Unit: rep'd for T.M. work. | |
| " | 7/11/17 | | Training. Weather showery. | |
| " | 8/11/17 | | Training. Weather fair. | |
| " | 9/11/17 | | Training. Weather fair. | |
| " | 10/11/17 | | Training. Weather showery. 1 Officer returned from hospital. | |
| " | 11/11/17 | | Weather improved. | stabs... |
| " | 12/11/17 | | Training. 1 O.R. to hospital. Received Bde Operation Order No 184. | |
| " | 13/11/17 | 7am | Brigade Tactical Exercise. Two gun teams with one gun attached to each Battalion. | |
| " | 14/11/17 | 7.10 | Brigade Tactical Exercise as before. Received 86 Bde Operation Order No I | attached |
| " | 15/11/17 | 7.00 | Brigade and other Teams with Battn and a shore guns and Teams | |

# WAR DIARY / INTELLIGENCE SUMMARY

Army Form C. 2118.

| Place | Date | Hour | Summary of Events and Information | Remarks and references to Appendices |
|---|---|---|---|---|
| BLAIREVILLE Corps H.Q. III | 15/11/17 | | 5 O.R. to III Corps School (or T.M. Course). Weather fair. Training. Weather bad. Preparation for move. | |
| | 16/11/17 | | | |
| | 17/11/17 | 21.30 | Left BLAIREVILLE for BOISLEUX & 0 NIGHT when the Battery entrained for PERONNE at 00.28. PERONNE was reached at about 6.30 and marched to HAUT-ALLAINE where it was accommodated in huts with the 86 M.G. Coy. | attached order |
| HAUT-ALLAINE | 18/11/17 19/11/17 | 9.15 | Battery marches from HAUT-ALLAINE to EQUANCOURT which was reached about 02.30. Rec'd R.O. Orders No 158. | attached order No. 17 |
| FRANCOURT | 20/11/17 | 2.30 | Battery less 1 Gun Team who were attached to R Battery moved into position into Brigade Reserve ready for the attack. Zero hour 6.20 x 3 hours. Advance was very successful. Casualties 2 OR: 11 wounded. 1 gassed and 1 O.R. – 7 MARTIN had over command of Battery in place of Capt HYDE wounded. Battery near H.Q. Moved to VILLIERS PLOUICH. | |
| VILLIERS PLOUICH | 21/11/17 | 19.00 | Battery Rear H.Q. Moved with Brigade to METZ EN COUTURE where we found the Reserve. At our Gun Teams. Enemy artillery fire normal. | |
| METZ EN COUTURE | 24/11/17 25/11/17 | 20.30 | At our Guns – ammunition and rations dumped. Left METZ EN COUTURE for MASNIERES where we were accommodated in Casemates. Enemy Artillery very active. Had 1 Gun in line in conjunction with 8 TM Bty. Enemy Artillery and machine gun active. Received 1 gun team from 89 Bty to replace casualties. | |
| MASNIERES | 26/11/17 | 9.00 | | |

# WAR DIARY or INTELLIGENCE SUMMARY

Army Form C. 2118.

(Erase heading not required.)

| Place | Date | Hour | Summary of Events and Information | Remarks and references to Appendices |
|---|---|---|---|---|
| MASNIERES | 27/11/17 | 9.00 | Guns attacked Rumilly on Fritillon. Had a premature which wounded 2 O.R. | |
| | | 15.30 | 2 Guns were blown up by enemy at 11 p.m. Commenced 9th Battery movement to G7H.S.G.&R.N.(I) (Horne Trench.) Received Orders to join at East-dan Road after night Orders carried out. Two O.R. wounded. Weather fine, formation heavily shelled. | |
| | 28/11/17 | | 1. Gun put out of action by enemy shell fire. 2 O.R. wounded. | |
| | 29/11/17 | 8.00 | Enemy opened intense bombardment and counterattacked getting a footing into Les Rue Vertes. Captain on commanding troops in these later they were driven off and we extricated 3 guns in those preceming. 1 O.R. killed 4 O.R. wounded. | |

C.V. Saggar Capt.

Brigade Major
86th Bde

> 88TH
> COMPANY.
> M.G.C.
> No... M.G. 3/23
> Date 21.1.2.17

Herewith war Diary of this
Unit for month of Decr 1917

Laurence Grady
88 Machine Gun Coy

# War Diary
## of the
## 86th Machine Gun Company
### Decr 1917

Vol.

| | Decr | |
|---|---|---|
| In the Line | 1st | The Company assisted in holding the enemy in his counter attack on MASNIERES.<br><br>During the night the village of MASNIERES was evacuated and the Company took up defensive positions around MARCOING<br><br>The following casualties occurred:<br>117235 Pte W Aspin<br>85224 W H Atkinson    2/Lt N Chivers<br>14309 T Raine    2/Lt A Lowe<br>114936 Ayers H.<br>210144 Hung T |
| | 2nd | The Company stood by for a further counter attack but were not called upon.<br><br>During this night the Company were relieved by the    Company & proceeded to billets in RIBECOURT |

The following casualties occurred
at [illegible]... [illegible]
[illegible list of names]

| | | |
|---|---|---|
| RIBECOURT | 3rd | The Company closed by executing orders. |
| | | Orders were received to proceed to camp at HAVRINCOURT WOOD |
| HAVRINCOURT WOOD | 4th | The Company proceeded by march route to FINS and encamped there. |
| FINS | 5th | The Company marched to ERVILLERS and entrained for PETIT HOUVIN |
| | | The Transport proceeded by road. |
| PETIT HOUVIN | 6th | The Company detrained at PETIT HOUVIN & proceeded by march route to billets at MAGNICOURT |
| | | The Company rested the remainder of the day. |

| | | |
|---|---|---|
| MAGNICOURT | 7th | The day was spent by the Company in cleaning up & a kit inspection. |
| | | The Transport arrived during the evening. |
| | 8th | The Company unpacked the limbers & overhauled all Gun Equipment |
| | | 2/Lt R. A. Latimer reported for Duty. |
| | 9th | The Company attended Church Parade. |
| | 10th 11th | The Company paraded at 9 a.m. & carried out programme of work as laid down |
| | | 2/Lt P. L. Strickland reported for Duty. |
| | 12th | The G.O.C. 28th Bgd. inspected the Company |
| | 13th | The Company paraded at 9 a.m. & carried out programme of work laid down |
| | | 2/Lt W. A. Brain reported for Duty |

| | | |
|---|---|---|
| MAGNICOURT | 14th | The Company carried out the programme of work laid down. The G.O.C 86th Brigade inspected the Transport. |
| | 15th | The Company packed all limbers preparatory to a move. Lt K M MOIR proceeded on leave to U.K. |
| | 16th | The Company proceeded by march route to BLANGERVAL and remained there for the night. |
| BLANGERVAL | 17th | The Company proceeded by march route to WAMIN and remained there the night. The roads were in very bad condition owing to a heavy fall of snow. |
| WAMIN | 18th | The Company proceeded by march route to SEHEN and billeted there. Owing to the bad state of the roads the Transport moved independently & were unable |

to get further than WICQUINGHEM

**SE'HEN** 19th  The Company rested in billets. The Transport arrived during the morning.

20th  The Company cleaned up, unpacked Timbers & improved Billets

21st / 22nd  The Company paraded & carried out programme of work as far as weather conditions allowed.
Capt J.P. Roberts proceeded on leave

23rd  The Company attended Church Parade

24th  The Company paraded & carried out programme of work arranged

25th  Christmas Day. A dinner was provided for the Company

26th / 27th  The Company paraded & carried out programme of work laid down

| | | |
|---|---|---|
| SEHEM | 28th | The Company paraded & carried out programme of work laid down |
| | 29th 30th | Orders were received from Div HQ that owing to heavy drifts of snow the road from SEHEW to HUCQUELIER would have to be opened at all costs. Church Parade was held in the evening. |
| | 31st | The work on the road was completed at 6pm & the Company rested the remainder of the Day |

Army Form C. 2118.

86 MGC

Jan - Feb 1918

# WAR DIARY
## or
## INTELLIGENCE SUMMARY

(Erase heading not required.)

86th Machine Gun Company (XXIII)

Instructions regarding War Diaries and Intelligence Summaries are contained in F. S. Regs., Part II. and the Staff Manual respectively. Title pages will be prepared in manuscript.

| Place | Date 1918 | Hour | Summary of Events and Information | Remarks and references to Appendices |
|---|---|---|---|---|
| SEHEN | Jan 1st | | The Company paraded at 9 a.m. and carried out Programme of Work as laid down. | |
| " | 2nd | | The Company paraded at 9 a.m. and cleaned limber afterwards packing blankets preliminary to moving. | |
| " | 3rd | | The Company paraded at 5.30 a.m. and proceeded by road route to SETQUES where billeted. Shot storm. Weather... | |
| SETQUES | 4th | | The Coy inspected limbers and cleaned along. Bells were fitted guns cleaned. | |
| " | 5th | | The Coy paraded carried out Programme of work. | |
| " | 6th | | Church Parade. Capt. Roberts reported for duty. Lieut R.M. West to Cavalry for course. Weather... Dull. | |
| " | 7th | | The Company carried out Programme of work so laid down for these days. Weather... Fine. | |
| " | 9th | | The Company proceeded to range carried out practices. The I.O.C. Brigade indented transport. Weather. Fine | |
| " | 10th | | The Company paraded and carried out Tactical Scheme. A practice advance guard was also carried out. The following awards were awarded in the Coy:- Capt J.P. Roberts M.C. 2/Lieut J.H. Rivers M.C. 2/Lieut A. Ashmore D.C.M. Lee/Cpl A. Young D.C.M. | |
| " | 11th | | Brigade Ceremonial Parade. Weather. Raining. Dull. | |

Army Form C. 2118.

# WAR DIARY
## or
## INTELLIGENCE SUMMARY.

(Erase heading not required.)

86th Machine Gun Coy.

Vol. XXVIII

| Place | Date 1918 | Hour | Summary of Events and Information | Remarks and references to Appendices |
|---|---|---|---|---|
| SETQUES | Jan 12th | | G.O.C. Division presented decorations to the New Years Honours recipients. Weather:- Dull. | |
| " | 13th | | Church Parades. Weather:- Fair. | |
| " | 14th | | Brigade Field Day. Limbers packed ready for move. Weather:- Snow. | |
| " | 15th | | Owing to rain vehicles were given to the Coy. The transport proceeded by road to BRANDHOEK. The Coy. Entrained at 4:30 a.m. and marched to WIZERNES where the entrained for BRANDHOEK - arriving in camp about 10 am. | |
| " | 16th | | The Coy. marched to JUNCTION CAMP in reserve Pte Nic Quade awarded the M.M. Weather: very wet. | |
| BRANDHOEK | 17th | | Guns etc cleaned. Trenches for the line. Weather:- wet. | |
| JUNCTION CAMP | 18th 19th | | Coy. relieved the 218th Coy. in the forward area. Rear HQ details. Transport moved into Camp at DEAD END. YPRES. | |
| " | 20th | | | |
| L. Mle Line | 21st to 23rd | | In the Line. Lieut. Coy. Relief was carried out on the night 24/25th. 64392 Pte G. France acc. wounded. 24th/1/18. 39049 Pte. S. Campbell wounded. 26/1/18 remained at duty. | |
| " | 28th | | The Coy. men relieved in the line and are conveyed by lorries to Camp at BRANDHOEK. | |
| BRANDHOEK | 29th 30th & 31st | | The Coy. rested. Cleaning camp, guns, equipment etc. | |

www.ingramcontent.com/pod-product-compliance
Lightning Source LLC
Chambersburg PA
CBHW080912230426
43667CB00015B/2661